MW01600601

TRUST YOUR TRU$T FUND

FINDING PURPOSE AND FREEDOM
WITH INHERITED WEALTH

TRUST YOUR TRU$T FUND

CHASE COLLINS

CHASE YOUR POTENTIAL

Chase Your Potential LLC
info@chaseyourpotential.com

ISBN: 979-8-9923859-4-6 (paperback)
ISBN: 979-8-9923859-1-5 (ebook)
ISBN: 979-8-9923859-2-2 (hardcover)
ISBN: 979-8-9923859-3-9 (audiobook)

Printed in: Charlotte, NC

Library of Congress Control Number: 2025906752

Ordering Information:
Special discounts are available on quantity purchases by corporations, associations, and others. For details, contact info@chaseyourpotential.com.

Publisher's Cataloging-in-Publication Data

Names: Collins, Chase, 1997- , author.
Title: Trust your trust fund : finding purpose and freedom with inherited wealth / Chase Collins.
Description: Charlotte, NC : Chase Your Potential LLC, 2025. | Summary: Provides advice for trust fund recipients and inheritors of wealth, allowing them to open doors of opportunity by having a purpose, a plan, and a grasp of financial literacy.
Identifiers: LCCN: 2025905595 | ISBN 9798992385922 (hardback) | ISBN 9798992385946 (pbk) | ISBN 9798992385915 (ebook) | ISBN 9798992385939 (audiobook)
Subjects: LCSH: Trusts and trustees. | Inheritance and succession. | Wealth – Management. | Finance, Personal. | BISAC: BUSINESS & ECONOMICS / Personal Finance / Money Management. | BUSINESS & ECONOMICS / Personal Finance / General. | BUSINESS & ECONOMICS / Finance / Wealth Management.
Classification: LCC HB715.C65 2025 | DDC 332.024--dc23
LC record available at https://lccn.loc.gov/2025906752

TABLE OF CONTENTS

Disclaimer i

Dedication iii

Introduction v

Chapter 1: My Family's Story 1

    Fighting Invisible Demons 2

    Family Dynamics 4

    The Loss of a Lifetime 8

    A New Reality 10

    Both Sides of the Coin 14

    My Inheritance 17

    Discovering Generational Trauma and Generational Healing 19

Chapter 2: The Psychology of Inherited Wealth 25

    An Emotional Burden 25

    The Best of Intentions 28

    The Inheritance Effect 29

    The Psychological Impact of Sudden Wealth 33

        1. Identity Crisis 36

        2. The Emotional Rollercoaster 37

        3. Relationship Issues 37

        4. Financial Management 39

        5. Loss of Motivation 40

        6. Unrealistic Expectations 41

    Affluenza 43

Chapter 3: Understanding Generational Trauma 47

   How Generational Trauma Manifests Itself 47

   What Is Generational Trauma 49

   Generational Trauma and Generational Wealth 53

   Signs and Symptoms of Generational Trauma 57

   Professional Treatment for Generational Trauma 61

Chapter 4: Releasing Guilt and Shame 65

   Recognizing Money-Related Guilt and Shame 65

   Other People's Stories 69

   Money Is "Evil" 71

   The History of Guilt and Shame 74

   Emotional Conditioning 76

   Impact of Unaddressed Excessive Guilt and Shame 77

   Leave Your Burdens Behind 78

   Steps for Overcoming Guilt and Shame 80

Chapter 5: The Power of Purpose and Fulfillment 85

   My Journey with Purpose 85

   The Power of Purpose 89

   A Guiding Light 93

   Discovering Your Purpose 95

   Purpose Evolves 97

Chapter 6: Financial Literacy and Management 101

   Don't Let Your Money Control You 102

   Having Money Doesn't Equal Financial Literacy 106

   The Five Key Components of Financial Literacy and Wealth

   Management 109

      1. Budgeting 110

      2. Saving 111

      3. Investing 111

4. Borrowing. 113

5. Managing Debt. 113

Financial Management for Inheritors. 114

1. Wealth Assessment 114

2. Creating a Budget 116

3. Managing Wisely 117

Grow Your Trust and Set Up Future Generations. 118

Chapter 7: Building a Life Beyond Money. 127

The Wheel of Life 128

A Rich Life 134

Cultivating True Wealth. 138

Conclusion. 141

Acknowledgments 145

Bibliography. 153

Endnotes 161

DISCLAIMER

The content of this book is for coaching and guidance purposes only. It is not meant to treat or diagnose anything, nor is it a substitute for professional medical, legal, or financial advice or counsel.

DEDICATION

To my dad and uncle. Thank you both for the endless love and light you brought to the world. The battles you fought allowed cycles to end and lessons to be learned. This book would not be possible without you both.

To my mom. You have been the best, most consistent, loving mother I could ask for. Without your love and support, I wouldn't be the man I am today and have the strength to follow my dreams. None of it would have been possible without you.

INTRODUCTION

Dear reader,

If you've inherited wealth and are struggling to find fulfillment and optimize your resources, take it from someone who has been there wandering aimlessly through life with a lack of purpose and what feels like wasted resources.

When the bills are paid and there isn't initial concern or worry about money, there can be a lack of motivation and drive to take action and create a living for yourself. This often results in drifting through life without direction, which leads to amplified addictive behaviors and impulsive decisions that aren't in your best interest.

As a life coach, I've had the pleasure of coaching a variety of people on an array of topics. I've worked in business coaching, men's empowerment, and divorce coaching. While I loved the work in each field, I wanted to focus on something that had a more profound meaning for me and the people closest to me. After witnessing multiple generations in my family struggle with their inherited wealth, I decided to help others navigate their inheritance and wealth so they didn't fall victim to the same pitfalls that repeat themselves in families with established generational wealth.

When I was a young boy, I watched my father struggle with addiction. I wholeheartedly believe this was due to too much money being handed over to him at a young age. This left him constantly wondering, "Why me?" and with extreme feelings of guilt, shame, and unworthiness. These left him in a vulnerable and unproductive state that seemed like a never-ending cycle until it killed him.

Growing up, I experienced the highest of highs and lowest of lows. Unlike my father—who grew up in pure abundance and was essentially set up for life—my siblings and I had more of a diverse experience. Up until the death of my father when I was 11, I didn't have much of a concept of money. However, after his death, money concerns arose for my mother and quickly trickled down to me. I watched her take care of us as we lived paycheck to paycheck, not always knowing where we would live. Yet, I also knew I had a "trust fund" with a very minimal understanding of what that meant.

The difference between my father's circumstance and mine was the fact that my trust fund was a great head start, but surely nothing that would set me up for life. This led me to figure out how to create a living for myself and find true fulfillment.

When asked about the perfect amount to leave one's children, Warren Buffett once answered, "Enough money so that they would feel they could do anything, but not so much that they could do nothing."[1]

This book covers the untold truths of inherited wealth, the many blessings and hidden curses that come along with this circumstance, and actionable steps to optimize your resources. By studying the psychology of generational wealth and trauma, managing your wealth, optimizing your wealth, and tapping into your purpose and fulfillment, you can create your own life completely independently of family wealth and expectations.

The only way out is through forging your own path and creating your own destiny. How will you change the world with the resources you've been gifted?

Sincerely,
Chase

CHAPTER 1
MY FAMILY'S STORY

"Dad, Dad? Wake up!" I shook him again and again, but he wouldn't wake up.

It was two in the morning, and my younger brother and I woke up in a fully lit, quiet hotel room where we intuitively knew something was wrong. We were there alone with our dad for a visit after our parents went through a separation. I was only seven years old, and this wasn't the first time I found my dad passed out from an overdose.

When my dad didn't budge, I looked at my younger brother. His eyes were wide and fearful. My heart raced as I scrambled around the room, searching for a phone to call my mom or 911. Coincidentally, I was just taught how to dial my mom on the cell phone the day before, but there were complications with the call and we couldn't get through to her. She had what she called "mother's instinct" and dialed us, already in the car and ready. In the back of my mind I prayed my dad would be okay, but I also knew deep down that he would be because this had happened before.

My dad went through a cycle that, even as a seven-year-old, I'd come to recognize. It involved him using drugs and alcohol, overdosing, going through treatment, and then going to rehab again.

I was too young to understand the depths of my father's pain and what led him to cope with drugs and alcohol. It was years later that I began to realize why he ended up on the path that led to multiple overdoses.

FIGHTING INVISIBLE DEMONS

My dad was the coolest, funniest, most humble, and down-to-earth guy. Everyone who met him loved him. He came from a wealthy family and grew up with privilege and luxury, but he was battling with invisible demons.

One of my favorite photos of my dad. That smile lit up every room he walked in.

My father grew up in an impressive family of achievers, but the wealth was inherited. His grandmother was heir to an oil and steel industry fortune. She created a family full of generous philanthropists, business owners, and artists alongside those who liked to "have a good time," which did not lead to the best outcomes.

He was the second youngest of six children, and he always seemed to be the glue that held the siblings together—everyone's favorite brother, son, and uncle. The family was very well off, and wealth was established three generations above him. Not only did he grow up in affluence and luxury, but he had peace of mind knowing that his children would have their own trust funds. There was also a lot of emotional neglect, being raised by a nanny quite a bit while his parents traveled to their winter home in Florida.

At 18 in the 1970s, my father was handed a big chunk of money—a couple million—enough so that with the right decisions he'd never have to work again. He was also told there was a lot more coming his way. As a young adult, he suddenly had the resources to do whatever he wanted, but he did what most young adults are advised to do without guidance or purposeful calling. Consequently, he left his home in the Chicago suburbs and headed to southwest Colorado for college.

Of course, college led him straight into the jaws of an intense party scene.

I don't think he knew it at the time, but as I grew up I came to realize that the cycle my father was in was deeply rooted in guilt and shame. He never understood why he had everything handed to him and never had to be without while other people struggled to put food on the table. But he tried to find ways to ease that guilt, and that was through his generosity.

We were at a carnival once, and my dad wanted a shirt to remember that day. He always bought T-shirts everywhere we went. However, the carnival didn't sell merch, so my dad decided to trade with one of the carnival employees. He took his shirt off his back and traded it for a shirt a not-so-clean worker was wearing. Throughout the entire exchange, he smiled and made friends with a perfect stranger—all to get a memorable shirt. I always saw him as a light-hearted, friendly, and kind-to-everyone guy, no matter their background or circumstances. That was my dad. He knew he wasn't better than anyone else, and all humans had the same inherent worth.

Due to my father's endless kindness, many people took advantage of him. They preyed on his guilt, shame, and wealth. I didn't understand it until I saw it myself, but it was always there under the surface, adding to his internal struggle.

Carrying his inheritance around was a guilty weight that kept dragging him down.

FAMILY DYNAMICS

Before my father met my mother, he was married and had children. From the beginning, I was surrounded by love and abundance, but a roller coaster of experiences also accompanied that.

I was raised in a big "modern" family. My father's ex-wife—my sisters' mother—was always there. They all managed to maintain a pretty good relationship for us kids. Overall, it was a great, big family dynamic.

At least, that's how it seemed when I was younger.

As I entered my pre-teen years, I started to notice more about my parents. This led to some strong, traumatic experiences that shaped me into the man I am today. I witnessed turbulent party habits and a self-destructive lifestyle that was funded by my father's family money. Neither of my parents was driven by the purpose of making a better life for themselves or us kids.

Our modern family. My dad, my mom, my brother,
both of my sisters, and their mom.

A family photo at my grandmother's house in Chicago.

I believe it was this lack of fulfillment and purpose that left my dad struggling with day-to-day life. I hate the word *addict*, but my dad was one. He wasn't the typical addict that might come to mind. The one thing I know about addiction is that nobody would choose it. He was nothing but fun, loving, supportive, and funny. There was only one time in my life when I saw him get mad. He was the best dad.

My dad and his four kids.

His charm and humor could move mountains.

Although that's the face he showed to the world, he desperately tried to numb himself from the guilt, shame, and painful memories from his childhood that he kept to himself. I do know that the loss of his second daughter when she was 10 days old contributed to severe levels of grief that he didn't know how to handle. Instead, he suppressed his sadness. From alcohol, pills, cocaine, weed, and nicotine, among others, he was in and out of rehab. And to pile onto his feelings of guilt, grief, and a direction-less life, he was constantly hounded by friends and family to get better. It was a never-ending cycle of attempting to get better and to live up to the expectations his family had for him.

Both my parents were heavy into the party scene, but it was clear my dad had more amplified addictions. By the time I was seven, I had witnessed a handful of overdoses. After 10 years, the rollercoaster of partying and addiction caught up to my parents and the marriage ended. My brother took the divorce harder than I did. Of course, it impacted me— as it would any kid—but I had been through so many other traumas that the divorce didn't seem like the worst of it.

Before they divorced, I remember my parents talking about moving away from Colorado to help my dad distance himself from the vicious cycle he was in. Unfortunately, we never made the move. After the divorce, my mother, brother, and I remained in our hometown in Colorado, but my dad knew he needed a change of scenery to stay away from partying. For a while, he bounced between his hometown in the suburbs of Chicago and Florida before settling in Chicago. He came back to Colorado frequently, and my brother and I would spend our summers and holidays with him.

My dad, my brother, and I.

THE LOSS OF A LIFETIME

When I was 11 years old and wrapping up my last weeks of fifth grade, I had an end-of-the-year project. The project was on my family tree. On Monday, May 18, 2009, I borrowed my mom's phone and called my father to get some information about his side of the family. He sounded deathly ill, although he assured me that everything was okay. He instructed me to call one of his brothers, who could provide me with the information I was looking for. As always, we exchanged "I love you's" and shared our excitement about seeing each other in less than a week to spend the whole summer together.

For some reason my mother didn't have my uncle's number, so my dad sent me his number and I called him to get the information for my project. The following day on Tuesday, May 19, I woke up as usual, ate breakfast, showered, and got ready for school.

While I was in the shower, my mother got a call from my uncle—the same one I spoke to the night before.

"David's gone," my uncle told her.

She let out a screech of anguish that my brother and I both somehow missed while we were focused on getting ready for school. It must have been a very hard morning for her, holding all that in for me and my brother and passing along that grievous news to other family members. She had to call my father's first ex-wife and give her and my sisters the tragic news.

Unsure of how to break the news, she put on a brave face and got us packed up for school. She also called our grandma—her mother—who came to our house right away. Just as we were about to get in the car, my grandma showed up at our house and my mom sat us down. "I need to talk to you two."

My stomach sank, and instantly I knew something was wrong. Until that moment, I hadn't noticed the distraught look on her face or how swollen her eyes were.

"You know how we always talk about angels and guides?"

My brother and I nodded.

"Well, God takes people from Earth when it's time for them to become angels, and last night was Dad's turn." She couldn't keep herself from crying, and I instantly fell into her lap in tears. My brother—who was only 10—didn't fully grasp the concept until I broke down in tears. The rest of that moment was a blur while we cried and tried to process the terrible news.

After so many years of addiction, he had finally landed on a good path and tried to stay away from drugs—especially painkillers. He struggled with pain in his back and gout and took ibuprofen daily. Unfortunately, there are potential side effects of taking over-the-counter medicines, and he developed a serious ulcer. This led to a catastrophic gastrointestinal bleed, and that was the reason he sounded so terrible when I spoke to him on the phone that last time. By the time medical help arrived it was too late, and my dad had already passed away.

The next thing I remember from that morning was staring blankly out the car window as we drove to my sister's house. I'll never forget the moment we all saw each other and collapsed in each other's arms.

As funeral preparations were being made the next week, we spent quality time together, shared memories and stories of my father, and instantly grew closer as a family. We'd always been a tight-knit family, but the death of my father allowed us to become closer than ever before. As we settled onto the flight to Chicago to go to the funeral, I sat next to my mother, looked over to her on my right, and said, "I'm not going to cry anymore. I'm done." And I never cried about it again. Not even at the funeral. I now know this was a block on my own grieving process that denied me the chance to process and heal from the loss. I have since done immense work to make it through this block and process my grief.

After the funeral, my family's level of stress reached a new level. My father and his family's money had been a major aspect of our financial support and what felt like stability to my mom.

A NEW REALITY

In the original divorce settlement, my mom got a chunk of money. It was enough for her to set herself up financially if she made good decisions with it. Unfortunately, she didn't have the knowledge or infrastructure to make that happen, so within a couple of years that money was gone—before my father's passing.

Being the oldest boy and sibling in the house, I grew up overnight when my father passed. I took on responsibilities no 11-year-old should ever have to take on. From then on, my adolescence became even more turbulent than the first part of my childhood.

My mom had already entered the workforce before my father's death, but now that she was raising us independently, there was a newfound pressure to pay the bills and take care of us.

I learned a lot of important lessons from growing up with a single mom. I watched her struggle, live paycheck to paycheck, move over 14 times, and experience all the other circumstances that developed as a result.

My mom, my brother, and I.

Unfortunately, my father's passing was not the only devastating loss I experienced in my youth. My father had five siblings, all with their own inherited wealth. Most of his siblings were able to manage their inheritance, seemed to lead fulfilling lives, and didn't struggle as much as my father.

However, his youngest brother and best friend, William, similarly struggled with what it meant to inherit such wealth and how to find purpose and fulfillment. Just like my father, Uncle Will was fun, cool, completely authentic, and the funniest person I'd ever met. They got along so well, as they were kindred spirits.

And just like my dad, my uncle had demons to battle. He came out of the closet at a young age and found his true love. He had a career that kept him occupied, at least for a short while.

My dad and my uncle Will, best buddies.

Will's long-term partner—my godfather—had AIDS. He was able to manage it with medication to live a long, healthy life—that is until a pharmacist mis-prescribed his medication and advised him to take too much. Will's partner was very suddenly taken in 2001, and my uncle was forever tortured by that loss.

Looking back, I believe that this was the beginning of the end for him. He'd always struggled with similar addictive tendencies as my father, but when he lost his partner it sent him into an out-of-control spiral.

In 2008, my grandmother passed away, which left my uncle even more lost and immersed in grief. Nine months after my grandmother passed, my father was gone. The two closest people to my uncle were no longer there for him.

In 2014, my Uncle Will passed away due to an overdose.

While we were booking flights to Chicago for the funeral, we got a call from his attorney. We were asked to extend our trip because we were in his will and needed to sort out his estate. My siblings, cousins, and I went to Will's house the day after his funeral. I couldn't stop staring at the couch he'd died on. It was very unsettling for me. The whole experience was surreal. We were given sticky notes and told to put our names on what we wanted to claim throughout the house. At 16 years old, it felt unconscionable.

I had a strong awakening at this moment. From the outside looking in, this was a big, beautiful, new house full of material wealth. It would be easy for anyone to think that he had everything and that his life must be perfect. Looking around, I saw a lot of material wealth that didn't make him happy.

There was overwhelming evidence of his drug use throughout the house, and I saw things a 16-year-old isn't meant to see. I'll never know the depths of his pain, but based on his addictions and quality of life toward the end, I know he was struggling immensely.

By this time, I'd seen the worst of what inherited wealth could bring to an individual and family. More than that, I started to see a pattern emerging, and it wasn't limited to my family.

BOTH SIDES OF THE COIN

While I never had to worry about money from my father's side of the family, the situation was very different with my mother. She supported us paycheck to paycheck, and her financial status constantly fluctuated. Sure, we had a roof over our heads and food in the refrigerator, but there were times when we lived in borderline poverty. My mother subconsciously projected a constant sense of stress about money onto me and my brother. My brother and I sometimes had to pull money from our own trusts to support basic needs. It was an odd experience to be 12 years old and emailing my trustee for cash.

Despite the ups and downs, my mother was the best mother she could be and was always there for us. She was truly the most consistent person in our lives.

Although raising us boys wasn't easy, my mother taught my brother and me many important life lessons during this time—many of which weren't conscious. One such lesson was about money, which humbled us and showed us a much bigger reality. Not only did we gain a drive and motivation to create the best possible lives we could for ourselves, but we also learned about the value of money. More accurately, the value of a dollar.

I knew from a young age that I had a trust fund. While that wasn't a big deal on my father's side of the family, on my mother's side it was seen differently. It was much harder for anyone to sympathize or relate, even though my brother and I never felt any different.

It was constantly being thrown in our faces that we were "rich" despite not having access to the money.

My mom, my brother, and I.

I can still feel the gut-wrenching feelings of guilt and shame when someone made a comment or gave me a look that told me they resented the fact that I had inherited a trust fund. It's a horrible feeling to be resented for something you have no control over.

By the time I was in high school, my brother and I took over paying the rent from our trusts. I've never had a problem with this, and I was grateful, though at the time, it was very confusing. To pay the bills in high school wasn't typical—but neither was having the resources to be able to.

From my first day of kindergarten, it was clear that I didn't thrive in a traditional school environment. My turbulent upbringing made my resistance to school even worse. After my dad passed away, I completely checked out in middle school. I always felt like I had too much to worry about when it came to money and financial concerns, and school didn't seem so important. I constantly felt like I was dealing with bigger, real-life issues.

Even though I didn't resonate with the school environment, I always liked to work. I started working on a ranch at a young age, and all through high school I worked at restaurants. I loved bringing home a paycheck, as it felt rewarding to me. That was something else I learned from life with my mom—how rewarding it was to make my own money and support myself. It was an important lesson I'd have to return to in adulthood.

I always knew I wanted to get out of my small hometown. After graduating high school, I went to Santa Barbara, California, for college. That lasted all of one semester before I knew it wasn't for me. I took an internship in London and quickly found myself thriving. I decided that my time in academia was over.

In the summer of 2017, after my semester in London, I was back in Colorado. I had many interests and opportunities to explore. I accompanied my best friend to real estate school. That summer—with the same friend—I attended a Tony Robbins event in New York, which was my first introduction to personal development and life coaching. That week really resonated with me and catapulted me into the coaching trajectory.

Learning from my uncle and my father, I knew I wanted to do something fulfilling with my life, but there were so many possibilities—almost too many.

At the end of that summer, an opportunity arose to work for my best friend's family business. After an unfortunate event within their family, his mother needed help in one of her art gallery locations. I immediately packed up my car and hit the road to Santa Fe, New Mexico. My friend and I were nothing more than two 18-year-olds running a multi-million-dollar art gallery—it was a pretty big break for us.

I knew this aligned more with my desire for a purposeful life than school. I was getting all the experience I needed in business and sales, interacting with people, and managing professional relationships. For a while, we worked six to seven days a week and we gave it 100%. Earning a paycheck that supported my lifestyle and paid my bills felt amazing.

There was a big difference in how I felt about the money I made versus the money I inherited.

MY INHERITANCE

My grandmother was a very wise, perceptive woman. She saw how the inheritance had impacted her family, and she realized that more structure was needed within the trust. I am forever grateful for the way she structured that money for me and my siblings.

Whereas my father got larger chunks of money in one lump sum, she planned to have chunks of our trusts paid out to us over a 14-year period starting at age 21 and ending at age 35. She wanted to give us a chance to be more mindful of our money and more responsible, too.

At age 20, I already knew how fast money could be spent. From watching my mother live paycheck to paycheck and noticing the spending habits I'd picked up myself, I knew I wasn't prepared to handle a substantial trust payout in one go. I've always loved fashion, traveling, and the finer things in life, and my credit cards reflected that. I knew I needed a plan for the payout as I approached my 21st birthday.

Back when I attended real estate school, I knew I didn't want to sell houses, but I also learned how great of an investment owning real estate could be. So, when my 21st birthday rolled around I decided to buy a home. With the decision made, I knew that it would be the best place for me to put my money.

Ironically, my financial advisors and trustees advised against it. They wanted me to keep that money in the market where I'd have access to it at my discretion or to take it out and live off of it. I'm glad I knew myself well enough to know that I couldn't trust myself with that money on hand. I proceeded to get my house, move in, and immediately feel it was my biggest accomplishment. It was an asset and investment that I couldn't spend impulsively but would still increase in value.

It filled me with so much pride to pay the mortgage and take care of it.

Less than a year later, I decided to relocate to New York City to pursue other dreams. I quickly transitioned from homeowner to landlord, turning my house into not only an asset but also a revenue source. Despite the other money I've spent, my house almost doubled in value and increased my net worth. Additionally, the income I made off of it as a rental property was enough to cover my rent in the places I've lived since. Five years later, at the time of writing this book, buying the house is still the best decision I've ever made.

While this real estate decision was the best for me, it isn't necessarily the right choice for everyone's situation. There are a lot of other options for increasing assets and generating passive income.

DISCOVERING GENERATIONAL TRAUMA AND GENERATIONAL HEALING

I was baptized Episcopalian, but my family didn't go to church on a regular basis. Even so, I can't remember a time when I wasn't spiritual. My dad was also a spiritual guy, always talking about his dad—who passed away more than a decade before I was born—and our other ancestors. His spirituality seemed natural, which translated well to us when we were kids.

After his passing, new spiritual doors opened up for me and my siblings.

My siblings and me in 2008.

My mother took my brother and me to a medium six months after my dad's passing. She told us it was a way to channel and connect with him. I was skeptical. It wasn't the easiest thing for me to wrap my head around.

Within five minutes of talking to the medium, she brought up an argument my brother and I had in the car on the way to the appointment. It was nothing she could have known or Googled to learn about. After that experience, I was convinced. My brother and I were captivated by what she had to say.

I've since worked with mediums and used them as a guide to help me through life. It was a way to feel connected to loved ones who have passed and look for messages they want to pass along. These messages have led me to a deeper understanding of money and wealth, especially as it relates to the experiences my father and uncle had.

Throughout my early 20s, I struggled. Even though I was well on my way to building the life I wanted, I still had a lot of healing to do and I knew it. Working with mediums was helpful, but it didn't go deeply enough, as I needed to heal on a more profound level.

My eldest sister is a naturopathic doctor. When I was 14, she mentioned alternative plant medicines to me when she learned about them in school. At the time, I was drawn to it but didn't understand the depth of the medicine.

It wasn't until many years later, during the 2020 pandemic, that I had the opportunity to work with a shaman. My natural spirituality and curiosity caused me to not think twice before going all in.

I had no idea what I was getting into with my first plant medicine therapy session. It was life-changing in ways that I never could have predicted. I walked away from that journey with a completely new outlook on life, and it's where I was first shown that I should get into the business of serving others. I wanted to start helping people. It was through this experience that I became aware of generational trauma and the cycles it creates.

Generational trauma, also known as intergenerational trauma or transgenerational trauma, refers to the transmission of trauma and its psychological effects from one generation to the next. This concept suggests that trauma experienced by individuals or groups in the past can have a lasting impact on the mental, emotional, and physical well-being of their descendants.

On my healing journey, I felt compelled to use other plant medicines as well. I went to a retreat in Costa Rica for a masculine-aligned plant that is said to heal up to seven generations of trauma and end those cycles for good.

During my journeys, I could see my family's empire being built. I uncovered the hidden truths of how a pattern of generational trauma related to inherited wealth had manifested itself within my family. I felt the power and the intention in this healing journey and the ending of cycles. This was one of the most difficult—yet most important—steps that I took for myself.

I had put up a lot of emotional walls years earlier when I told my mother I wasn't going to cry about losing my father anymore. Going through these alternative medicine journeys broke through the walls I'd built around my grief and allowed me to process it. I worked with an integration coach who helped me process the plant medicine and everything that had come to light. All the generational curses, cycles, and traumas were clear, and it paralyzed me for months.

Not everyone will feel called to use plant medicine, and it certainly is not for everyone. This was an important part of my healing journey. It led me to some of my most eye-opening revelations into inherited wealth, its links to generational trauma, and the deeper psychology of inherited wealth that inspired me to help others so they wouldn't have to struggle with the guilt and shame that ultimately took my father and uncle.

After becoming conscious of my family's generational trauma, I immediately understood my father and his daily struggle more than I had before. It changed the way I thought about money, wealth, and inheritance.

While on my healing journey, I could look at myself, my father, and my uncle with much more clarity. I've seen money come and go. I've been in the unique situation of living in both abundance and scarcity. I've had the beautiful experience of figuring out how to support my desired lifestyle long term because my trust fund isn't going to carry me through my entire life. I've used my trust fund as a crutch in the past, taking advantage of the money because it is there. I've also asked myself, "What if I never had this? What would I have already created or accomplished with my same lifestyle desires?"

I'll never know the answer to those questions. However, the experience I've had with my inheritance pushed me to find a life of purpose and fulfillment, and to go after what I wanted, which I think my father and uncle lacked.

In 2021, I decided to cut myself off from my monthly distributions for the year ahead. It was an interesting test for me, and what happened was truly fascinating. Without hesitation, I sent the email to my advisors and was fully committed to the decision.

After just two weeks of cutting myself off, I came upon an opportunity that replaced the income my trust fund was providing for me to the exact dollar amount. It was like the universe's way of showing me that I would always be taken care of, and I got a front-row seat to the law of sacrifice in action. This law states that you have to let go of something of a lower nature to gain something of a higher nature.

Working for my money, earning it, and respecting it was of a much higher nature to me.

I felt like this was my first real step to creating a healthy relationship with money, a lesson that not everyone who inherits or comes into money is able to receive. For this reason, it's a lesson I want to share so that those in similar situations who might be less fortunate can benefit from it.

For more customized tools and resources on loss, inheritance identity, grief, addiction and more, visit trustyourtrustfund.com.

CHAPTER 2
THE PSYCHOLOGY OF INHERITED WEALTH

A fact of inheritance that I had to learn for myself, and one I learned through talking to members of my family and others with similar circumstances, is that when people inherit money they face challenges unique to their circumstances—challenges people outside those circumstances don't understand. Through my personal journey, I reached out to others who inherited wealth—some in my family and some outside my family—and I discovered that many of these challenges could be placed into two categories: financial and emotional.

AN EMOTIONAL BURDEN

Sudden wealth syndrome is identified as the stress, guilt, social isolation, and confusion that accompanies a sudden, large windfall. This could be in the form of an inheritance, selling off a business, winning the lottery, or receiving a pro athlete's salary at a young age. While it isn't a psychological diagnosis, psychologists like Stephen Goldbart—who coined the term—have studied how it has impacted those coming into large wealth that lasts for years.[2]

One of the most significant financial challenges facing people who inherit wealth is how to preserve and grow their wealth. Many of them don't understand the value of a dollar—nor do they have any financial planning experience—so they can quickly spend it all without having any way to get it back. It's a more common problem than people realize.

The emotional burden of inheriting wealth involves keeping our lives on track, dealing with friends and family reactions to the inheritance, and managing the impact that kind of money can have on one's life.

At times, inheriting money can feel more like a burden than a blessing, and without the right support and consultation it can stay a mixed blessing—leading to guilt, shame, confusion, and a risky lifestyle.

Turning inherited wealth into a full-time blessing is done by taking a balanced approach—being smart about money while taking good care of ourselves.

When I read the following story about Jim in Street Directory, it reminded me of some of my own challenges and experiences with inherited wealth—challenges I've heard again and again as I've talked to other people in the same situation.

Jim grew up in an affluent family where their wealth came from real estate. His dad was also a prominent attorney who represented the interests of wealthy people in their communities. Like many inheritors and children of affluence, his life was planned for him. He was essentially given two career options: law or business. The goal was for him to take over and work in the family business. That's a lot of pressure for someone to grow up with and live up to. It isn't uncommon in wealthy families for these kinds of expectations to be imposed on kids at a young age.

Unfortunately for the family, Jim didn't want to go into law or business. He loved music and started playing piano at age 12. Eventually, he moved on to writing songs, singing, and performing. After high school, despite his father's discouragement, Jim went to Los Angeles to pursue a career in music. His father thought he was throwing his life away and was disappointed that he wasn't taking up the family business. Again, that kind of pressure and expectation can be very damaging and traumatic for anyone to go through, and they fought about it a lot. Tensions rose even more when Jim came out to his family and introduced his partner to them.

When Jim turned 25, he came into his inheritance from a trust created by his grandfather. He decided to call a consultant to help him manage his life and newfound wealth. Sadly, a lot of people in Jim's situation don't have that foresight and their lives go in totally different directions.

Jim wanted to focus on his relationship with his father and learn how to manage his wealth. His consultant began working on the psychological and emotional side of things, helping Jim separate himself from his father's expectations and disappointments. This gave him a better understanding of himself and, at the same time, his dad. He was able to recognize the family expectations his dad was pressured into. In doing this work, it gave Jim a totally different perspective about his dad and why he was the way he was.

The other part of this work was ensuring Jim knew how to optimize his inheritance while also having a healthy relationship with his money. He decided to pursue his music career further by going back to school. At that time, Jim was struggling with his partner, who expected Jim to take care of him because of Jim's financial circumstances. It was a rough time for them, but eventually they came to an agreement that felt good for everyone.

When someone inherits wealth, it is common for their friends or spouses to feel some kind of entitlement. I've had friends and even family try to make me feel guilty for not spending more on them or helping them out more "just because I can." I imagine Jim felt very conflicted and guilty about how to handle his partner's expectations of being supported financially.

Jim was able to use his inheritance for a fulfilling, purposeful life. He used his money to follow his passion for music, develop boundaries, improve his relationship with himself and with others, and set himself up for financial security. By taking on the financial and psychological issues that come with inherited wealth, he turned what was first a burden into a gift.[3]

THE BEST OF INTENTIONS

They say that the road to hell is paved with good intentions. When senior family members give wealth to the next generation or generations, it is always done with the best of intentions. Whether it's through ownership of a family business or other assets, the goal is always to give future generations a leg up.

The trusts set up for my father and his kids were meant as just that.

While it's always done with good intentions, unfortunately these gifts are set up through elaborate trusts and estate plans that are driven by the Internal Revenue Code (IRC). In the long run, doing so doesn't take the well-being or benefit of future generations into account. A common theme in setting up generational wealth is that matriarchs and patriarchs, often through the guidance of their advisors, focus more on minimizing tax consequences than on long-term considerations.

These inheritors, who are given this gift with the best of intentions, end up fighting an uphill battle on multiple fronts. On the one hand, there are family expectations to live up to by becoming some kind of "business hero" that upholds the family name and reputation. On the other hand, to people without money we're seen as "silver spoon" kids, and our talents and efforts are hardly recognized while we are told that we're handed everything from birth. It is a strange place to be in the middle. It can feel like you're being torn in two. I think that's how my dad felt a lot of the time.

The technical term for this phenomenon is called the *inheritance effect*. It is defined as "the very real consequences that can arise from inheriting business wealth rather than earning it through personal investment or sweat equity."[4]

The *inheritance effect* can lead down two paths. The first occurs when the inheritor feels pressured and forced into working hard only to prove their worth and contribute to their family business—not because it aligns with their values or because they truly want to do it. The second path is one of discouragement and lack of motivation, which will ultimately prevent the inheritor from taking any action at all and will cause them to fall into a trapped mindset. Both of these can occur at the same time, making the *inheritance effect* even more complex.[5]

THE INHERITANCE EFFECT

After losing my father and my uncle at a young age, I went through a lot of personal development and spiritual journeys. They led me to insights and realizations about inherited wealth within my family and other families that I couldn't ignore anymore.

It was mind-boggling to me to witness all this happen and for no one to talk about it. Within my own network, it wasn't something that was brought up at all. Outside my network, there was the stigma that "silver spoon" kids are spoiled and nothing is ever wrong in their lives. I was surrounded by skeptics, which presented its own set of challenges.

No matter where I turned, I felt like my mental health was being brushed aside. There was this idea that because I had a trust fund, I must not have any problems. I had money, so I'd be fine. There was another idea surrounding me that since I had money and resources, I was always able to take care of anything that was wrong, so there was no need to address mental or emotional health if it was already being handled.

I thought there had to be other people who were aware of these patterns and struggles, so I started researching. That's what led me to the *inheritance effect*, and suddenly, it was all there in black and white: the truth. Just reading about the *inheritance effect* and learning more about it validated my feelings and gave me a sense of hope and comfort, knowing I wasn't alone.

What I discovered was that, at its core, "the inheritance effect is the result of short-sightedness."[6] What makes it complicated is that it isn't intentional short-sightedness. No one who sets up generational wealth thinks that the process is undervaluing the emotional or psychological impacts it will have on the next generation. Unfortunately, that is how it plays out a lot of the time.

One thing I first experienced when I was in high school and using money from my trust to help cover living expenses is that the money never felt like it was mine. I've spoken to my siblings and others about this, and they experienced the same feeling. It felt like we were using someone else's money, so the expectation was to use it for something meaningful or in alignment with the values of my advisors or trustees. That's why one of my older sisters used her trust to put herself through medical school.

Oftentimes, inheritors do not feel like the owner of their assets. Someone else created the empire. It belongs to them, and it is up to us not to make the wrong decisions and lose it all for future generations. Not only is that a huge expectation to carry around, it almost puts a limit on us in terms of what we can accomplish.[7]

An ancestor created such great wealth for the family—how could any of us ever surpass that? What's the point in even trying?[8]

Falling into that thought pattern—combined with the fact that as a gift there is no personal accomplishment for receiving that wealth—a lot of inheritors never feel the need to attain anything for themselves.

That's not to say inheritors don't try to attain their own wealth or grow their family legacy. Unfortunately, those who try also run into their own wall of challenges. From within the family, they are unlikely to be noticed or recognized for their hard work and accomplishments. They are held to the standard of those who came before them. Every action and step is judged, whether successful or not. Sometimes, they are diminished for misusing the gift they were given.[9]

From outside of the family, their accomplishments can be diminished further because all people see is the trust fund behind them and assume that every accomplishment they've made is based on their privilege and not their talents or hard work.

This leads to further feelings of guilt and anxiety about money, personal identity, and capabilities. My cousin told me, "I had major guilt and anxiety over having to ask the bank just to transfer money to my checking account. It made me feel like I could not support myself—like I was inadequate at being a capable adult. I could never ask my husband to pay for everything. I have this weirdness about saying I need money. It's just easier for me to figure it out, even though it's not really. Having a job makes me feel like I'm doing my part and contributing even though it's lots of extra stress that I currently don't love or need. But I get up and do the damn thing every day!"

There's a well-regarded thought in the psychology world known as loss aversion. People, in general, have a greater fear of losing what they have than a desire to gain more. The gift of wealth becomes "a responsibility to look after"—a burden that comes with guilt.[10]

William Kissam Vanderbilt, third-generation descendent of Cornelius Vanderbilt, once said, "My life was never destined to be quite happy… It was laid out along lines which I could not foresee, almost from earliest childhood. It has left me with nothing to hope for, with nothing definite to seek or strive for. Inherited wealth is a real handicap to happiness."[11]

While intended as a gift, inherited wealth comes with a power structure that can be psychologically damaging to inheritors. When assets are set up in trusts, the founder chooses how to divide up the ownership before the transfer is made. Usually, these decisions are made when later generations are very young or before they are even born—long before the inheritors show their true potential.[12]

From the founder's perspective this approach ensures they have more control over the assets and is designed to prevent misuse by the next generation. Unfortunately, this can backfire, as it can freeze the inheritors into a sociologically stunted place with trustees. As a result, inheritors feel infantilized due to the lack of trust in managing a sizable asset or become consumed with fear of failure.[13]

Personally, I think this is where the "rich party kid" stigma can stem from. If someone is treated like an untrustworthy child long enough, they start acting like one. To top it all off, ownership influence doesn't carry over to the next generation. Just because the assets are legally owned by the next generation, they're usually disregarded and brushed off as silver spoon babies—even by the corporate leaders of any family business. They aren't respected as owners, and their authority isn't trusted. Beneficiaries of a trust with non-voting shares hold the least amount of ownership influence. In the long term, this can be severely damaging to both next-generation family members and the business.[14]

Sometimes, generations that are even further removed from the founder are "forced into passivity 'for the good of the business,'" as the adage goes.[15]

"There are obvious upsides to a life born into immense wealth, but the prospect of inheriting unimaginable sums can strain personal relationships, erode self-confidence and trap a person in a near-permanent state of dependence," say therapists and wealth advisors who work with ultra-wealthy heirs, according to a *Washington Post* article by Leo Sands.[16]

THE PSYCHOLOGICAL IMPACT OF SUDDEN WEALTH

Inheriting a large sum of money can be both exhilarating and overwhelming. My two older sisters didn't know they had trust funds until they were in their late teens.

My oldest sister has expressed how she felt she needed to spend her trust fund on college and education. Even though that's not written within the trust, she always felt an unspoken expectation that she had to spend it on college, so she went to medical school and spent upwards of $500,000. She is now a rare, debt-free practicing naturopathic doctor, and for that she is grateful.

On the flip side, my brother and I knew that we had trust funds from a young age. I don't remember how old I was when I found out, but it seemed like I always knew. Sometimes, I wonder how different my life would be if I hadn't known until I was older.

Outside of my family, I've spoken with other inheritors who have experienced sudden wealth and discussed how it impacted their lives.

I first met Brittney when I began my coaching journey. Her story instantly captivated me, and I found that I shared a lot of her feelings even though our experiences were wildly different.

Brittney grew up in a family where her mother inherited wealth. She watched her mother live off her inheritance. Even from a young age, she knew she didn't want to live like her mom or manage money like her.

She received a lot of mixed messages about money from her mother, which contributed to feelings of confusion about money, inheritance, and wealth. Her mom was very careful with her money. Maybe too careful. While cautious money management isn't a bad thing in itself, the problem Brittney had was that her mom never believed she could make money herself.

She saw her inheritance as her only means of survival, so she never aspired to do anything with her life and never really "lived" because she was worried she'd run out of money.

In her early adulthood, Brittney came into an inheritance of about one million dollars.

Shortly after inheriting her money, Brittney was drawn into a cult. People who join cults are often vulnerable in some way. Whether it was because of her inheritance, her relationship with her mother, or her views on money, there was something that made Brittney vulnerable.

It's possible they saw her as an easy mark because of her inheritance, as it isn't uncommon for young adults or recent inheritors to be targeted and taken advantage of with their newfound wealth.

After joining the cult, Brittney gave every single penny of her trust to them. She was able to get out but never got her money back. When I asked her if she regretted giving her money to them, she said no.

I was a little thrown by that answer, so I dove a little deeper. Brittney told me that she chose to give her money away to the cult. Not because she was taken advantage of or brainwashed or anything like that. She said, "I gave it away because I didn't want to be like my mom, and I knew I could go on and make my own money."

Brittney had a solid idea of what she didn't want in life. She didn't want to limit herself and her ambitions. She didn't want to resign herself to living off her inheritance. She didn't want to give up on what she sought to accomplish just because she had doubts as to whether she could make it on her own.

Giving her money to a cult set her free. She never regretted it and spent the next 25 years focused on building her own career. Now, she has a business generating over $50 million in revenue. On her own, she was able to accomplish far more than her trust fund ever would have given her.

Brittney's story, like mine, shows that sometimes money can hold us back. But when we proactively cut ourselves off from it, we find the time, motivation, and ability to do even greater things with our lives.

In the grand scheme of inheritance, Brittney is a bit of an anomaly, as most inheritors don't have such a clear vision or path to follow. Still, Brittney faced the same challenges all inheritors face. She just went about resolving those challenges in a unique way.

The Money, Meaning & Choices Institute coined the term *sudden wealth syndrome* to describe the challenges that inheritors face. These challenges include stress, confusion, and money mismanagement.[17]

One group of people the MMCI looked at more closely was professional athletes. In 2022, the average starting salary of an NFL player was $2.7 million, and the lowest starting salary of any NFL player was $705,000.[18] That salary usually increases through the course of their career. And yet, 78% of NFL players are bankrupt or experiencing financial stress within two years of retirement. Within five years of retirement, 60% of NFL players are bankrupt or broke.[19]

Most pro athletes are young (some in high school or college) when they get drafted and have no experience handling money. They get used to it always being there until it isn't, and they don't know how to maintain it when that money isn't flowing into their account.

There are six major challenges that inheritors face when coming into a sudden inheritance of wealth.

1. Identity Crisis

My father is an example of someone who struggled with this a great deal. There were times he followed certain paths. He thought it was expected of him, whether it was what he wanted or not because he didn't have a solid grasp on his own identity.

Whether you're suddenly thrown into a world of luxury and privilege after not experiencing it before, or all of a sudden given a large sum of money that you haven't managed before, it can all be head spinning. If you did grow up in luxury and abundance, that large sum of money is at major risk of loss based on the lifestyle you're accustomed to. It challenges existing beliefs, values, and relationships, and makes one question their self-worth and purpose in life, which can all lead to questioning one's identity and create feelings like they don't belong.

2. The Emotional Rollercoaster

There is an emotional rollercoaster ride that inherited wealth takes us on. This rollercoaster is severely underestimated and misunderstood by most people. There can be a lot of excitement and joy at first. A "dream come true" feeling. But after the initial excitement fades, feelings of guilt, anxiety, and even depression often creep in.

This is the "why me?" feeling my dad had. He saw all the people around him, around the world, struggling with basic human needs, and he wondered why he deserved this wealth that he hadn't worked for, while other people continued to struggle. This had a ripple effect on the rest of his life. Being taken advantage of, partying, overspending, divorces, etc.

On top of guilt comes fear. A lot of inheritors fear losing or mismanaging the money, which causes increased stress and anxiety. This pressure, in some ways, becomes like a self-fulfilling prophecy, as a lot of inheritors try to soothe that stress with pleasure spending and partying and can even fall into different addictions where they burn through the money faster. This only perpetuates that fear more, and it eventually becomes a cycle.

3. Relationship Issues

The third challenge that comes up is trust issues. No one likes to think money can change a relationship, but it does happen. Just like Jim's partner felt he should support him because he had the means, that kind of sudden wealth can drastically shift relationship dynamics. It can cause issues to arise between family members, friends, business partners, and romantic partners.

Several years back, my brother and I went in together on a used car for my mom. She needed a car, so we found a good deal and decided to give her one as a gift. I'll never forget one of my aunts commenting about us getting her a used car and how we should have bought her a new one because we could afford it when, in reality, she had no concept or context of our financial positioning.

Comments, assumptions, and entitlements like this can negatively impact relationships and lead to trust issues. It made me wonder whether giving a gift would always be met with that kind of remark because people assumed I could afford better, so I should be giving better. But doesn't that taint the very nature of gift-giving?

Sometimes, inheritors can feel like people are only interested in their money rather than a genuine connection. I know inheritors who have unintentionally isolated themselves because of these kinds of trust issues and have had trouble forming authentic relationships. It can be very lonely, especially in a world where, even among inheritors, these challenges aren't openly discussed. It can feel like we are traversing these thoughts and experiences alone, and something is wrong with us because we're the only ones who seem to be struggling.

When I was 16, I encountered my own violation of trust that resulted in legal repercussions. I had just received my driver's license, and a "family friend" who knew of my trust fund asked whether I would house-sit while they were on vacation. They set me up to stay at the house, stocked the fridge, and made me feel welcome. Although they said I could, I didn't sleep there once. I did my duties daily and spent minimal time there. It was the end of the school year, so as high school students we were excited for summer and celebrating. On a Friday evening while they were gone, I had seven friends over to the house before we went to a party. Everyone was respectful, and nothing was damaged or stolen whatsoever.

When they returned home, I got a scathing call accusing me of misconduct that never occurred. They oddly knew more than was humanly possible, which led me to assume they were watching me on a camera. Looking back, it seems like they planned this from the start. I was disciplined for having the seven people over. I apologized, as that was a mistake on my part, and moved on with my summer.

Three months later, as I was getting ready for school, there was a knock on the front door and I answered. They asked whether I was Chase and if my mother was home. I got my mother, and to our surprise we were served papers. They were suing me.

This entire situation was blown out of proportion. They clearly had ulterior motives. In the court documents, they claimed we damaged and stole upwards of $7,000. There were insurance claims and falsified "proof" of these claims.

After all was said and done, after a few court hearings they essentially won, and I had to pay their renter's insurance deductible. They filed for insurance—fraudulently—and got $7,000 in insurance money from their renter's insurance company.

This was a wild experience for a 16-year-old. It really awoke me to the ulterior motives people have and the true intentions of everyone around me. It was clear I was set up and taken advantage of. I couldn't believe that anyone would sue a 16-year-old. It was one of my first lessons in how willing people are to take advantage of people with money for their own gain.

4. Financial Management

Any sum of money needs financial literacy and discipline on the part of the owner in order to preserve and grow it, whether it's a hundred extra dollars on a paycheck or a sizable inheritance. Many people assume that because inheritors have money, they know how to manage it. Just because we were given this gift doesn't mean that we have an innate knowledge of effective management. Many inheritors have no knowledge or experience in managing their wealth.

It's true in any financial bracket that poor money management can lead to stress, anxiety, and long-term financial difficulties. Inheritors aren't immune to that. In fact, they can sometimes be more prone to it. If they've been surrounded by money and wealth their whole lives, they have no understanding of how fast money can be spent or what the value of a dollar is. And if no one is looking out for them to teach them money management, they won't know it's a necessary part of managing their new wealth.

In my personal experience, I've felt very detached from money. I also think this makes spending and "blowing" it easier. I've always had the feeling that the money wasn't mine, and when I ask for money, it feels as if I'm asking someone for a loan or to give me their money. When I was working, I noticed different spending habits and feelings around the money I earned versus the money I had been given.

My dad had a humorous quote he would say to us kids. "Let's go spend some money." This shows he had the same detachment I've experienced with the money. But when the money won't hold you over for life and is nothing more than a head start, every dollar counts toward the life one may desire for themselves.

5. Loss of Motivation

When money is not a concern, people can lose meaning and lack direction. My father went to college because "that's what people do." Because this was his sole reason, he never truly had direction or purpose for his life, which led him to the never-ending party scene.

Without the need to work, people can feel like they are just drifting through life. When I moved to New York, I wasn't working and was relying solely on my trust fund to pay my bills. I was in a part-time design program at school, but I wasn't taking action. I had my own desire to create and try different things for my career, and I wanted to earn money doing something I enjoyed. There was no clear path or direction for me, and I wasn't pursuing anything.

I experienced that same directionless feeling again a few years later when I first set out to start my own coaching business. I knew I wanted to coach men who were struggling with their sexuality and identity, but for six months or so I sat around with the idea without taking action. There were multiple factors causing my inaction, but I think one of the most prominent factors was that I didn't need to take action in order to pay my bills because my expenses were covered, and I was comfortable.

Without that need, there was no sense of urgency to follow through on my desires or goals, which made them easier to put off.

6. Unrealistic Expectations

As a whole, society romanticizes the idea of wealth. It's the solution to all of life's problems. People say, "If only I had a million dollars, I could do so much with that," or "If I could win the lottery, I'd never have to worry about anything again."

A common adage explains that money can't buy happiness. And yet, when someone receives a large inheritance or sum of money, they can often feel disappointed or unsatisfied when that money doesn't bring instant happiness, solve their problems, or make life's challenges go away.

A Princeton University study from 2010 concluded that money contributes to happiness as long as it is covering basic needs. But for people earning well above that threshold, having more money didn't increase their happiness. Additionally, money could support happiness by protecting people from things that make them unhappy, like an expensive divorce or other unhappy and potentially costly life experiences. While there is some correlation between money and happiness, it caps after basic life needs are covered. From there, having more money doesn't increase happiness.[20]

In 2018, another study looked at 4,000 millionaires in the U.S. to determine their happiness and satisfaction levels. That study found that at the basic millionaire level, there wasn't a notable difference in happiness between average earners and millionaires. The biggest difference in happiness for millionaires was in those worth over $10 million. Even then, the satisfaction and happiness of decamillionaires wasn't significantly greater than regular millionaires.[21]

To top it all off, that same 2018 study found that those who inherited their fortune were less happy than those who worked for it and earned it.[22]

Even regarding lottery winnings, there are plenty of studies to support the idea that money isn't a driving force behind happiness. A study from 2007 showed that lottery winners who won around $200,000 were greatly stressed in the year they won. After two years, that stress leveled out and they were happier than they were before.[23] A follow-up study in 2018 concluded that even if moderate winners were a little happier after that first year, it didn't last because the lifestyle impact of a moderate sum isn't very big. That 2018 study also found that for winners of larger prizes, there was no increase in happiness.[24]

So, while money may have very loose ties to happiness, it has nothing to do with the amount of money and more to do with whether or not your basic life needs are comfortably covered financially. This is a common misconception that a lot of people, even inheritors, still struggle with.

AFFLUENZA

It has been well documented in the psychology community that wealthy people often lead lives of chronic anxiety, depression, and underemployment.[25] This often starts out in adolescence and childhood when children in wealthy families are at a higher risk of experiencing boredom, isolation, and depression because there is a culture of idleness in wealthy youth.[26] Early childhood experiences can contribute to feelings of emptiness and low self-esteem that carry into young adulthood and beyond. In many wealthy families parents are often busy and rely on nannies or live-in help to raise their children, and there are typically no expectations for teenagers to work. As a result, children may grow up feeling unimportant to the key figures in their lives. This sense of insignificance can lead to lingering low self-esteem.

My father often felt more of a maternal connection with his nanny than his mother because she had a more active role in raising him. That pattern persists in many wealthy families.

Psychology has termed these various pathologies *affluenza*. It is defined as dysfunctional relationships associated with wealth. Affluenza includes a lack of motivation, an inability to delay gratification or tolerate frustration, low self-esteem, and increased susceptibility to addictions to alcohol, drugs, and/or gambling.[27]

I've seen many of these traits reflected in people around me—my father, people in my family, and even some of my wealthy friends. My dad struggled with multiple addictions, and he wasn't the only one in my life who did.

In these instances, wealth often feels like a burden.

Of course, not everyone born to wealth experiences affluenza, and some want to deny that affluenza is even an issue. However, some inheritors have acknowledged the concerns around affluenza and have taken action to do something about it.

The term *affluenza* was popularized by psychotherapist Jessie H. O'Neill, founder and developer of the Affluenza Project, who defines the term as "a dysfunctional relationship with money/wealth, or the pursuit of it." She elaborates her definition by stating the following: "The collective addictions, character flaws, psychological wounds, neuroses, and behavioral disorders caused or exacerbated by the presence of or desire for money. In individuals, it takes the form of a dysfunctional or unhealthy relationship with money, and may manifest as shame, guilt, anger, rampant materialism, hoarding and/or all manner of addictive/compulsive behavior."[28]

The Affluenza Project offers a wide variety of services.

Part of the mission is to raise public awareness and promote healing. There are others in the psychology field also working to combat affluenza. One technique used relates to how wealthy parents can handle incidents that their children get into, which mitigate the development of pathologies associated with affluenza.

For example, if a teenager repeatedly wrecks their car, the solution shouldn't be to buy them a new one just because the money is available. Parents should talk to their children about what happened and set boundaries, like having them get a job to make monthly payments on their next car.

An approach like this helps teach wealthy children responsibility, curbs instant gratification, and encourages them not to be idle and to work for what they want, whether the financial need is there or not.

Affluenza is prevalent among wealthy families, especially those with generational wealth. However, more initiatives are being provided to help treat and prevent it.

We are all subconsciously taught by watching how our parents operate as we grow up. We also inherit generational trauma and cycles that play a role in both our parents' actions and our own actions.

So, coming after generations that had been set up for life, seeing their spending habits taught me that money comes and goes. With that belief, it's been difficult to be held accountable when it comes to my spending habits.

More times than I can count, I've overspent, over-invested, over-indulged, and ended up with large credit card bills and/or unnecessary debt. Unlike a working-class person who has to logistically figure out a circumstance like this and be held accountable for the nature of making and spending money, I've always had my trust fund as a scapegoat.

My unhealthy spending habits were solved with a simple email, which resulted in a cycle of overspending, over-investing, and overindulging.

For my entire life, I've had a deep-rooted core belief that money only comes from one place—my trust fund. I believe this has slowed me down in earning the money I want independently. This has been shown to be untrue based on my job history and resume. I've made a living for myself and made money elsewhere, but I still had this underlying deep belief that abundance and money only came from my trust.

My trust fund has allowed me to live a lifestyle that I wouldn't be living in my 20s if I didn't have it, which plays into my belief that I was incapable of creating this lifestyle, income, and abundance for myself. Also, seeing other people, family, and friends go through their inheritance and have to start from ground zero instills a belief that it's only temporary and "that's how it goes."

Until I started researching the psychology of inherited wealth, I didn't realize how much research had been conducted on the subject. Since the early to mid-1900s, this topic has been studied by a handful of people, with research proving the major emotional and psychological effects of inherited wealth.[29] It was somewhat comforting to see the research, as I felt my experience and the experience of my family were validated.

This was all the more encouraging for me to start talking about it and to create a service that tackled the very issues of this circumstance: guilt, shame, boredom, assumptions, stigmas, addictions, lack of motivation, family expectations, aimless wandering, etc.

For more customized tools and resources on the
Psychology of Inherited Wealth, visit trustyourtrustfund.com.

CHAPTER 3

UNDERSTANDING GENERATIONAL TRAUMA

My dad, growing up in the affluence that he did, had a live-in nanny whose name was Ella. Although my dad spoke highly of his parents, I sensed that he had wounds that stemmed from being raised primarily by Ella. When my mother first met the family in Chicago, he introduced my mom to his mom, then when he introduced her to Ella and said, "Now this is my real momma."

While it isn't uncommon for wealthy families to employ nannies, in my father's case I think it led to unspoken feelings of abandonment and complicated questions my dad never got answered about his own identity and his role in the family. This was just one layer of the wounds and trauma my father experienced growing up and is an example of the lowered self-esteem due to a family life in which a child never feels significant to anyone, referenced in the previous chapter regarding symptoms of affluenza.

HOW GENERATIONAL TRAUMA MANIFESTS ITSELF

In the two generations above my father, all the money came through the women—his grandmother and his mother. So, enter the men they married, my great-grandfather and my grandfather.

My grandfather did what he could with the resources my grandmother brought to the table. Wheelin' and dealin', as they'd say. He had several business ventures, but there's one that stands out more than the others. He got involved in a real estate development in the Chicago area that had a promising return on investment. It was supposed to be a guaranteed return.

When it all went down, he lost upwards of 30 million dollars.

That was money my grandparents were never able to recover or make up with any of their other business ventures.

I don't know the logistics of everything that occurred, but I do know my grandfather took the blame and never forgave himself. I can't imagine the pressures of losing an amount that large. It was something that forever changed their lives and the future of generations to come. My grandfather ultimately died of a heart attack, and I'm sure this deal affected his health overall.

To this day, I'm not entirely sure how that impacted the trusts set up for my dad's generation and my generation that followed, but I do know that was a lot of money to lose. At the time of the real estate deal, my dad and his siblings were old enough to learn about their own inheritances and to be aware of what was happening.

Watching someone lose that much money in one deal was no doubt a traumatic experience for my father and his siblings. I imagine it influenced a lot of the decisions they made about their own inheritances and how it should be spent or not be spent.

Experiencing or witnessing a major loss like that is considered trauma.[30] And while my dad didn't live through that loss himself—he didn't make the deal or the investment—he still experienced it firsthand by watching his dad go through it.

According to an article published by PsychCentral, non-biological trauma can be passed down from one generation to the next through dysfunctional dynamics between family members, family stories of traumatic events, memories, photographs, heirlooms, and letters.[31]

There are both physiological and psychological components to generational trauma, which can make it harder to identify or trace the source.

Given that my dad and his siblings saw the real estate deal go wrong, I've questioned how it affected them and their relationship with money. I mentioned that my dad seemed to be detached from the money he inherited. I think that deep down this deal instilled a fear in my dad and his siblings that forever deterred them from taking risks when it came to investing their own money.

My siblings and I are also familiar with the story, and it has served as a cautionary tale—but that goes to show how even a story can have a ripple effect through generations.

This kind of major impact event is called generational trauma. And sadly, it isn't uncommon in families that have established multiple generations of wealth.

WHAT IS GENERATIONAL TRAUMA

By definition, generational trauma—sometimes called intergenerational trauma—means the passing down of traumatic experiences from one generation to the next.[32] These types of trauma are usually the "result of direct personal experiences, witnessing acts of violence, or residing in environments where the threat of violence is ever-present."[33]

According to *Psychology Today*, "epigenetics is the study of how the environment and other factors can change the way that genes are expressed." Epigenetics doesn't change the actual gene sequence, DNA, or genetic code, but it can inform development.[34]

The study of epigenetics has found that certain traumatic experiences can impact the chemical compounds attached to different DNA sequences. It is the science of how generational trauma can be perpetuated beyond the generations that experience the trauma firsthand.[35]

Many times, people are oppressed and mistreated. What I found intriguing when I first started to learn about generational trauma and cycles was the fact that my dad, grandparents, and I didn't necessarily have these specific circumstances that cause generational trauma. In fact, it was the complete opposite. We were wealthy, white, and privileged. But nevertheless, I found myself healing deep generational wounds that felt heavier than a million pounds of bricks. This led me to question things about my family lineage and gave me a better understanding of my dad and the demons he struggled with.

I was first able to confront and start healing my generational trauma when I went through an alternative therapy program that employed the use of plant medicine and holistic options. This particular program was intended to heal trauma going back seven generations. When I first learned about this form of therapy, I immediately had a gut feeling that I needed to do it because of my tumultuous family history.

I dove into research mode and started to learn about generational trauma. The more I learned, the more I saw how it had seeped into my family and influenced my life, my siblings' lives, and especially my father's and uncle's lives.

I learned that this type of trauma is psychological and may result in physical and mental health issues, as well as social and emotional challenges.

An example of generational trauma would be someone growing up in a home with domestic violence. Witnessing violence in childhood can lead to depression and anxiety in adulthood, along with trouble forming intimate relationships. The cycle continues in the next generation of children growing up in a home environment with depressed, anxious parents who have trust and intimacy issues.[36]

With each generation of unresolved trauma, new traumas and symptoms develop and get passed on to the next generation, oftentimes getting more and more amplified and destructive.

This means that even if someone doesn't directly experience domestic violence or witness it, they can still suffer from it. People who have directly experienced that trauma raise and interact with their families based on that trauma. In some cases, people with unresolved trauma turn to substances as a way to block it out, and their children learn not to talk about their feelings, perpetuating the cycle further.

Fortunately, it is possible to heal generational trauma.

With the right support, treatment, and patience, family patterns can be broken. In my journey through alternative therapy, I saw images of my family building their empire, and I was able to go back in time to have conversations with myself as a young boy, my parents when I was younger, and my parents in the present day. Yes, even my deceased dad. Although my actual journeys went well, I got home to New York City and immediately was hit with overwhelming sadness and grief, falling into what seemed like never-ending tears. It was the first time I really cried and grieved my father's death since telling my mom I wasn't going to cry anymore after he passed.

As part of this treatment, I had an integration coach to help answer my questions and guide me through the period immediately following the program. I hopped on my first call with my integration coach and was completely lost in trying to process the feelings of grief and sadness that surfaced. Along with the grief I was processing from 11 years of not allowing myself to, I released something way bigger than myself and events that didn't directly affect my generation. At the time of getting on this first call, I had no idea the depths of what I was processing and releasing for my family and generations to come.

Before I could even say anything, my coach started crying and emotionally purging for me. She sensed my pain and took it on herself, releasing it through her own tears. Afterward, she said, "I'm happy I can take some of this off of you. I haven't encountered something this heavy in I don't know how long."

Over the next 90 minutes, I had one of the biggest wake-up calls of my life. While I'd been introduced to the concept of generational trauma, cycles, and healing before, with this call I started to become more conscious of my own generational trauma, allowing me to work toward releasing it.

I was awakened to the deep, dark, unspoken secrets of my family and started to understand the depths of my dad's pain and the vicious cycle he was stuck in. Everything started to make sense—why he was the way he was, his habits, his unattachment from the money, etc. It led me on the healing journey of my life and has brought me many beneficial insights into generational wealth's link to generational trauma.

GENERATIONAL TRAUMA AND GENERATIONAL WEALTH

Because of the stigmas surrounding generational wealth and inheritance, it can be difficult for others to view the life of a trust funder as traumatic. As a result, the trauma and emotions surrounding inheriting aren't talked about openly—even among inheritors.

These results can stem from the idea that because inheritors have money, they have the resources to take care of their mental and emotional health—a common misconception I mentioned previously. Similarly, when people think of "trauma," they think of domestic violence, sexual assault, witnessing a crime, and other violent or horrific events.

Inheriting a large sum of money doesn't fit in with those experiences.

Rahkim Sabree, a certified financial education instructor and author of the book *Financially Irresponsible*, said, "Generational trauma is arguably the biggest impact on our relationship with our finances. Often we learn by observation and reenact the things we saw our parents and grandparents do when it comes to the ways we think about, or even what we believe is attainable, with our finances."[37]

There are a lot of ways to be traumatized, and in a world of wealth, luxury, and complex family dynamics, those traumas might be subtler than other traumas but are nonetheless damaging. When family money and complex family dynamics collide, a perfect recipe for generational trauma is created.

Generational wealth and the accompanying traumas form an intricate web of interconnected experiences, each contributing to the next in a cycle that spans generations. Unrealistic expectations often accompany the inheritance of substantial wealth, burdening heirs with the weight of familial standards and traditions. The pressure to conform to these expectations can lead to emotional distress and a pervasive sense of inadequacy, creating a breeding ground for generational trauma that echoes through the lineage.

Family conflict further exacerbates these tensions, particularly regarding matters of inheritance and wealth distribution. Disputes within families can fracture relationships, resulting in long-lasting psychological repercussions for all involved. The unequal distribution of wealth only serves to deepen these rifts, fostering feelings of injustice and betrayal among family members who perceive themselves as unfairly treated.

I spoke to an estate planner who had direct experience handling and planning estates and trusts, but still viewed them from an outside perspective and had a unique take on the psychology that goes into setting up trusts and inheriting.

Jeremy primarily works on will drafting, trust drafting, and powers of attorney. He also works with financial planners, other professionals, and family members to get things in order. Because of Jeremy's background, he also works in estate litigation. He told me that when it comes to estate management, no one wants to end up in front of a judge—whether it is dividing up property or assets that have been forcefully inherited, challenging wills, or any other questions that come up after someone has passed and their estate needs to be managed.

As an estate attorney, a lot of his work overlaps with real estate and family law. He has had many experiences with estate planning, settling disputes over inheritances, carrying out wills, etc. I asked him about challenging wills, and he told me that 90% of the time, if there's a dispute it is usually because one person rightfully or wrongfully has taken control—not necessarily through the courts but through the family, and they may be doing what's legally allowable or not.

Jeremy said that in one case he was asked by another attorney to be an independent trustee because three siblings were accusing each other of manipulating their dad. He would oversee the money so that there wouldn't be any loyalty to anybody other than to the father.

Financial dependence on family resources can also contribute to the perpetuation of generational trauma. When individuals rely solely on familial support, their autonomy and self-sufficiency may be stifled, leading to feelings of helplessness and a lack of personal achievement. This dependency can become a vicious cycle and be passed down through generations, perpetuating the trauma associated with financial instability.

The weight of legacy and the pressure to uphold familial standards further compound these challenges. Inheritors may find themselves sacrificing their own dreams and aspirations in the pursuit of maintaining the family name, leading to excessive stress, anxiety, and resentment. Witnessing the misuse or mishandling of family wealth only adds to this burden, as future generations grapple with the consequences of financial mismanagement.

Emotional attachment to wealth can also contribute to generational trauma, particularly when it becomes the sole measure of self-worth and happiness. Inheritors may struggle to form meaningful connections or pursue fulfilling careers, trapped in a cycle of materialism that offers little in the way of true fulfillment. These values, inherited from previous generations, perpetuate the cycle of trauma, creating a legacy of emotional pain and insecurity.

In response to these challenges, individuals may develop unhealthy coping mechanisms, such as excessive spending or substance abuse, as a means of numbing their emotional pain. These behaviors, learned from previous generations, only serve to perpetuate the cycle of trauma, further entrenching the link between generational wealth and generational trauma. Breaking free from this cycle requires a concerted effort to address these underlying issues and forge a new path rooted in resilience and healing.

Jeremy told me that if there's a bunch of money going to people who don't have a lot of money, there's a lot of strife because everyone wants a large piece. If there's a bunch of money going to people who already have a bunch of money, it creates a whole different kind of strife because they have the money to pay for attorneys and litigation. They can pay to fight for it. He said that the person who dies is like the point of a triangle that holds everyone else together. Once they pass, it cuts those ties and changes the way people act. They're thinking, "Grandma won't get mad if I do X, Y, and Z because she's not here anymore." And that opens the door to a lot of complicated, risky behaviors and the manifestation of trauma.

I don't want anyone to think that all inherited wealth is bad or that all families who have generational wealth are bound to experience generational trauma. Family money can be advantageous for educational opportunities, philanthropy, promoting family well-being, and personal development.

I talked to Jeremy about the goals he sees when people come to him to set up trusts. He says the most common goal is to protect the future impact of their death on their children. With older or wealthier people, that sometimes extends down to grandchildren and great-grandchildren, which is what happened with my family. The intention is almost always to ensure the well-being of future generations. The roots of inheritance are good intentions, making them a valuable resource when the dynamics are better understood.

Chloe B. McKenzie, the founder of the Center for Financial Trauma & Wealth Justice, posited that financial generational trauma is the cumulative result of, or response to, harm done to a person's ability to build wealth and their overall relationships with money.[38]

Feeling ashamed of money or believing you're bad at managing it may be a sign of generational financial trauma.[39]

Some families grow closer through inherited wealth and family legacies. I know my siblings and I have very open, honest relationships that may have never developed if we didn't have a sensitive topic like our inheritance to talk about, relate to, and cope with one another.

By employing open and honest communication relating to financial matters, estate planning, and seeking professional guidance when needed, a lot of the negative effects can be mitigated for a healthier family environment.

Like other traumas, the way a family is impacted by generational trauma can vary significantly from one family to the next. Talking about money-related trauma and the psychological aspects of money and inheritance is essential for breaking the cycle of generational trauma caused by inherited wealth.

When I've started these conversations with my siblings, other family members, and acquaintances, I've realized that we've all been feeling it— we just haven't been talking about it. But now that we are, I think there is room for all of us to heal and build healthier relationships with money.

SIGNS AND SYMPTOMS OF GENERATIONAL TRAUMA

If generational trauma exists that stems from inherited wealth, the signs and symptoms won't necessarily be traceable to an obvious event or group of events. There probably won't be a noticeable history of oppression or violence cropping up in the record books. Identifying this kind of generational trauma can be challenging because it often manifests itself in subtle and complex ways.

Here are some common signs and methods for identifying generational trauma:

- Family patterns: Family patterns of abuse, neglect, substance abuse, mental health issues, or dysfunctional relationships that have persisted across generations can be indicators of generational trauma.
- Family history: Does your family history include major traumatic events, like the bad real estate deal my grandfather was involved in? If so, that trauma could be passed down from one generation to the next. Learning about the past can provide insights into the intergenerational transmission of trauma.
- Repeated negative outcomes: If multiple family members experience consistent challenges or negative outcomes over the course of several generations, including financial troubles, addiction, or problems forming healthy relationships, this is a sign that generational trauma is at play.
- Unexplained emotional reactions: Pay attention to strong emotional reactions, triggers, or unresolved feelings that seem out of place. Strong emotions and reactions can be learned from the stress and anxiety of parents, who can learn it from their parents, perpetuating generational trauma.
- Family secrets and taboos: I've mentioned before that in my family and other families I know with established generational wealth, talking about money, grief, and mental health was almost taboo. Anything a family doesn't want to discuss or pretends doesn't exist, can be a result of generational trauma.
- Beliefs and values: Generational trauma can influence beliefs and

values within a family. Consider the beliefs, values, and attitudes held within your family. Sometimes, this can bring negative self-perceptions and unhealthy coping mechanisms that are passed down.

- Transference of roles: Generational trauma can also be found in the transference of roles. If the same roles are being transferred from one generation to the next, this can be a result of that persistent trauma.

- Intergenerational communication: One thing I wished I had done more frequently when I had the chance was to talk to my grandmother and some of the older generations. Knowing more about their experiences could've helped unveil hidden trauma that had the potential to cause a ripple effect.

- Emotional resilience: You can learn a lot by taking a look at the coping strategies of other family members and their emotional resilience. Those who have experienced generational trauma will show it in difficulties handling stress, regulating emotions, and managing relationships. If you see any of these, there's a good chance generational trauma has been passed through your family.

- Mental health issues: Some mental health issues that manifest themselves from generational trauma include depression, anxiety, and post-traumatic stress disorder (PTSD). If you see a pattern of these issues recurring in your family or in your own life, then generational trauma may be at play.

- Professional help: Healthcare professionals, therapists, and counselors can be trained in identifying and healing generational trauma. There are also alternative therapies like the program I went through. Talking to someone can help identify whether there is persistent generational trauma and help you with a plan to break the cycle.

- Self-reflection: Engage in self-reflection and consider your own experiences and emotional reactions. Recognizing how generational trauma may have influenced your own beliefs and behaviors can be a crucial step in identifying its presence.

When you look for signs of generational trauma, it is my recommendation that you approach your investigation with sensitivity and compassion. Discussing and addressing these traumas within a family can be challenging. There are a lot of emotions attached to them, and if it is something that has been largely ignored or denied, then it could be difficult to discuss.

To break the cycle for yourself and future generations, you'll want to handle any difficulties with care and bring in professional help when needed. Even if other people in your family aren't ready or willing to embark on the healing journey, don't let that hold you back.

There are many outward, easily recognizable symptoms of generational trauma that can manifest themselves. I saw many of these in my father and experienced a lot of them myself as I struggled to make sense of my own feelings relating to my inheritance and the demons my father carried around.

As one Dr. Reshawna Chapple said, "The symptoms of generational trauma include hypervigilance, fears of death or no hope for the future, mistrust of outsiders, anxiety, depression, panic attacks, post-traumatic stress disorder (PTSD), low self-esteem, issues of addiction, domestic violence, and sexual abuse."[40]

According to Chapple, some of the common symptoms of generational trauma include:

— Anxiety
— Depression
— Chronic pain
— Substance abuse disorders
— Eating disorders
— Post-traumatic stress disorder (PTSD)
— Insomnia

— Low self-esteem
— Fear of death
— Irritability
— Anger issues
— Difficulty trusting others[41]

Licensed mental health counselor and financial therapist Aja Evans says that kids learn how to interact with money based on how their parents talk about it and interact with it. That cycle then moves from one generation to the next.[42]

Some signs indicative of financial generational trauma are:

• Overworking in an attempt to gain recognition, validation, and change financial situations.
• Overspending to numb emotions and temporarily ease pain.
• Avoiding accountability and action when it comes to reviewing finances.
• Excessive frugalness from a place of scarcity and fear of financial risk.
• Guilt and shame around financial positioning and personal wealth.
• Lack of motivation and drive to pursue your own career and life.

I'd like to note that these symptoms not only stem from generational trauma, but they can be strong indicators of it. If you see patterns of these symptoms across different branches of your family from different generations, then it could be related to generational trauma, and you may want to look into seeking professional services to help unravel it.

I know that for me, it was absolutely life-changing to confront the generational trauma and begin to heal from it.

PROFESSIONAL TREATMENT FOR GENERATIONAL TRAUMA

Most of the time, generational trauma goes untreated.[43] This is especially true when it is linked to inherited wealth. A lot of people don't associate wealth with trauma, and as I've mentioned before, there's the stigma that money and resources can fix anything. Considering those factors, I think that most families with established generational wealth never even consider generational trauma as a problem.

Of course, almost anyone will tell you that the first step to overcoming a problem is admitting that one exists. There are a lot of professional options available for identifying and healing generational trauma. They include generational trauma-trained therapists, coaches, counselors, psychotherapists, and other healthcare professionals with the right background.

These are all steps toward breaking the cycle of generational trauma, but they aren't the only ones. When I went on my journey with alternative plant-guided medicine, it gave me a lot of answers and insights, but I still needed to learn how to cope and manage what I was feeling and healing from on a day-to-day basis.

Some common coping mechanisms that can be used to manage generational trauma while you're going through the healing process include:

- Recognizing and understanding the impact of past traumas on your life.
- Exploring your family history and learning about the experiences of previous generations to gain insight into your own situation.
- Engaging in self-care practices.
- Building connections with people who have had similar experiences and can empathize with your struggles.

- Consulting a mental health professional if you're finding it difficult to manage your emotions or cope with challenges.[44]

Addressing your own mental health through whatever channels feel right for you and taking care of yourself physically, mentally, and emotionally are all integral to healing past wounds and breaking the generational cycle. I found the method that works best for me, and since then I have undergone a personal transformation that has led to me following an entirely new path that I'm excited about, and the same could happen for you. This book wouldn't have been possible without my own healing journey.

For more customized tools and resources on
Generational Trauma, visit trustyourtrustfund.com.

CHAPTER 4

RELEASING GUILT AND SHAME

When it comes to feeling guilt and shame, sometimes these emotions can be attached to a single, life-changing event that can easily be traced or tracked. When it comes to the guilt and shame surrounding inherited wealth, it's more subtle. It can't always be associated with a single event. Instead, it is more common that these feelings are woven throughout everyday experiences and interactions.

My dad's guilt and shame relating to his inheritance came from his own feelings of being undeserving. Many inheritors—when they don't earn the money themselves—can feel like they don't deserve it because they didn't work for it.

It can be hard to understand those feelings and where they stem from, or even put them into words.

RECOGNIZING MONEY-RELATED GUILT AND SHAME

My dad's guilt around his inheritance led him down a self-destructive path with substance addictions. More than that, he became a prime target for so-called "friends" to take advantage of. People asked him all the time to borrow money that they never got around to paying back.

This is one of the sources of mistrust for people with inherited money. They don't always know if people truly like them or just see dollar signs.

On the flip side, my dad's guilt made it a lot easier for him to part with the money—even if he was mistrustful of someone or didn't know them that well. After all, his own words were, "It's just money."

I don't think he associated his feelings of guilt and shame with the ease with which people took advantage of him. But I do remember one time when a couple borrowed $10,000 from him and actually paid it back. It meant the world to him because he was so used to handing out money without any expectation of repayment.

That one moment really stood out to my parents because other people never felt the need to pay my dad back. It was as if they assumed he didn't need the money or wouldn't miss it.

Even though my dad was blessed financially, he dealt with money stress his entire life. I believe that a lot of it came from underlying feelings of shame and guilt that influenced a lot of his financial decisions and attitudes toward money.

What a lot of people don't realize is that just because inheritors have wealth, it doesn't mean there aren't subtle money stressors that they have to cope with. The outward signs of guilt and shame might not be there or be related to a single impact event, but they still feel guilt and shame related to money, status, and inheritance throughout their lives. That's what my dad experienced.

An article for *Psychology Today* talks about "thriver's guilt" relating to survivors' guilt. The article, titled "How the Rich Cope with Shame About

Their Unfair Advantage," says that those living with wealth, and thus thriving in many aspects, feel guilty and shameful for thriving in a world where so many aren't.[45]

This is similar to how survivors feel after accidents and disasters, as they often question why they survived and are alive while others in the same situation are not.

People with thriver's guilt sometimes pretend they are self-made, which in essence denies their true feelings. Denial is one of the ways people cope with thriver's guilt, whether through ignoring it completely or pretending they are someone they aren't.

In my own experience, my guilt and shame came from comments other people made about my financial status. I grew up hearing comments and having judgments thrown at me about my trust fund and wealth. It always made me feel shameful for having this money, even though it was beyond my control.

People always seemed to judge my spending habits. In their opinion, I was either spending too much or not enough. I grew detached from my money in a similar way that my dad did, and I made a lot of impulsive purchases and wasted money on bad decisions.

While the spending might have felt good in the moment, it always left me feeling guilty afterward, like I was wasting this gift.

Sometimes, the guilt and shame associated with inheritance come from an external source, like your environment.

I had a conversation with my brother and he said something that brought up another source of guilt and shame for himself. He followed my lead and purchased a home when he received his first trust payout at 21.

Because he was in college at the time, he had friends and other college students move into his house and pay rent. None of them came from wealthy backgrounds or had trust funds.

The people he was closest to didn't understand his circumstances. This perpetuated his feelings of guilt over having something they didn't. Sometimes, because of these feelings he felt uncomfortable in his own home.

I've been very fortunate to be surrounded by entrepreneurs and business owners who understand money and abundance, which has created a more positive environment for me. However, there's one phrase I've heard frequently which can come from anyone in any situation and almost always causes feelings of guilt and shame to bubble up.

The phrase "You're lucky" carries a lot of weight for inheritors. For my entire life, people have told me I'm lucky because of my trust fund. It goes back to the assumption that money is the answer to every problem, and because I have money I shouldn't have problems. The catch-22 is that when someone says "You're lucky" but you don't feel lucky, you start to question a lot of things. It can make you feel guilty for not feeling lucky or for having struggles in your life—whether it's relationship struggles, career, financial, or mental health.

At the same time, you can feel blessed. Both terms indicate a positive event or situation where something good has happened to a person. Whether you feel lucky or blessed, the end result is typically favorable—such as receiving an opportunity, achieving success, or avoiding something negative.

Feeling blessed typically implies that a higher power or divine influence has granted you some form of favor or positive outcome. It carries a sense of gratitude toward something beyond yourself, such as God, the universe, or fate. Being "blessed" often conveys that the good things happening are not by chance but result from something purposeful or intentional.

Feeling lucky suggests that random chance, luck, or coincidence has led to your good fortune. There's usually no implication of divine involvement or purpose, but rather that you happened to be in the right place at the right time. Luck is often seen as unpredictable and can go either way—good or bad.

I mentioned before that it felt like people in my life brushed my mental health away because I had money and resources, so what could I have to complain about?

When people tell me how lucky I am, I think about this great blessing and the complicated feelings surrounding it, and I wonder why I am not happy with this amazing gift.

Guilt and shame can come from both internal feelings and external perspectives, which make them particularly difficult to avoid or ignore.

OTHER PEOPLE'S STORIES

Trust funds are designed to provide financial security and privileges to inheritors. They are meant to allow people to get ahead, live in abundance, and make a life for themselves. Just like my father, there are some who struggle with their inheritance and often fall into very miserable lives as a result.

Many trust fund recipients have talked about feelings of guilt and shame, feeling isolated by their money and subconscious collaboration with the world's corporate problems.

Lane Fury of Seattle, Washington, shared that she's received $185,000 from the family fortune and is going to inherit nearly six million dollars. She was quoted saying, "I don't actually want it. There is this sense of shame or embarrassment, like maybe some of the problems in the world are my fault, so I shouldn't really be open about [my wealth]." According to the *Daily Mail*, "Fury says a trust fund can spur feelings of loneliness, guilt, depression, and confusion. While there's comfort in financial security, it is also alienating."[46]

Trust fund recipient Adam Roberts, age 34, said his one million dollar inheritance makes him feel guilty. "I remember getting the trust statement when I graduated from college and seeing that I had ExxonMobil and Chevron stock—at a time when I was learning about climate change and the ways these large corporations exploit people and the planet. My first reaction was to disassociate and compartmentalize…I experienced longing to be less isolated in this experience, and for a world in which there weren't these huge differences between people."[47]

Robin Lee Allen, a 24-year-old from Brooklyn, shared that his wealth created a rift between him and his friends and family. Following a split from his father and the death of his mother when he was eight, he went to live with relatives in Tallahassee who had less financial means. By the time he turned 18 he had access to an amount "under five million," but he eventually depleted it.[48]

"I was very irresponsible. A lot of parties, a lot of travel, fancy, needless s***, like getting clothes custom made. A lot of taxis. It was just me trying to be a socialite…The money wasn't infinite," he said.[49]

Five years later, he faced near homelessness and found himself in a transitional housing program in New York City. Eventually, a compassionate couple from the Upper East Side offered him a place to stay. He went on to attend college and is now a managing partner at a private equity firm.[50] "I couldn't talk about so many other issues that I was facing with most people, so it wasn't until I [met them] that I realized there are lots of people [like me]," he shared.[51]

There are many reasons why guilt and shame are associated with money. Some of them come from internal feelings, but most tend to come from the external stigmas of what money and privilege mean.

A coach specializing in financial psychology named Derek Hegen talks about how these feelings of guilt and shame are "more common among the children of financially successful people." He says this is because their inheritance "feels more like a handout." Gaining status and a certain standing in society through inheritance and family connections can feel like something they don't deserve or didn't earn.[52]

MONEY IS "EVIL"

Some schools of thought relate money to the root of all "evil," and I often see in my daily life different societal portrayals of how money is perceived by either those who don't have it or those who want to influence how other people feel about money.

Many of those creating or inheriting wealth today were raised when influential segments of society, such as religious groups and politicians, began openly condemning wealth—especially great wealth concentrated in the hands of a privileged few.

Even today, popular culture's portrayal of the wealthy as inherently corrupt or insensitive can trigger feelings of guilt or shame.

For example, the wealthy understandably feel ambivalent when watching movies that portray affluent characters as villains, such as Cal Hockley from *Titanic,* Shooter McGavin from *Happy Gilmore,* or Jeffrey "the big Lebowski" Lebowski from *The Big Lebowski.* Although these characters do act a certain way, these movies and many others teach audiences to perceive people negatively simply because they have money. The language and images that politicians and the media use to broadly stereotype "the rich" would not be tolerated if they were directed toward members of an ethnic, racial, or minority group. We are certainly not a protected class under the law or in the media.

Often, money is seen as seductive, alluring, fascinating, and highly desirable. It's true that having money can create greater opportunities, but it also makes some people feel very alone and awkward.

Those who harbor deep feelings of regret, guilt, and shame about their money may fail to enjoy it and take advantage of the opportunities it provides. Such feelings frequently go unrecognized or unacknowledged and are thus rarely discussed openly with advisors or even family members. Yet, consciously or unconsciously, feelings of guilt and shame can dramatically influence wealth management decisions, as I've seen in very different ways throughout my family.

Wealthy individuals with these feelings sometimes give family members or charities more or less than they might genuinely want to provide. For example, a wealthy family leader once talked of his regret about withholding lifetime gifts to his children that could have helped them build their own careers and businesses out of concern that others might view him as being irresponsible and his children as spoiled.

Conversely, some parents who inherited their wealth express feelings of guilt for giving their children too much money out of the sense that they didn't really deserve it. The same is often true in philanthropy. Some wealthy individuals reluctantly make charitable gifts anonymously to avoid a reputation for flaunting their wealth. In contrast, others give very publicly—at times beyond their comfort level—to prevent the perception of being selfish or greedy.

Beyond societal pressures, people may experience feelings of guilt or shame because of the source of their wealth. For example, it is well documented that inheritors can experience low self-esteem, lack of motivation, and guilt. As Lane Fury and Adam Roberts expressed, the source of their wealth also filled them with guilt because of larger implications like environmental impacts and feeling like their families and they were partially to blame.[53]

Some who inherit wealth feel ashamed of receiving handed-down wealth because they have so much and feel inadequate compared to the family members who made the fortune.

Furthermore, children of affluence are often afforded special treatment simply because their families have money, a reason they intuitively know has nothing to do with who they really are. Some inheritors even act out the negative behaviors that they are taught to associate with being wealthy.

One individual who joined a successful family business and struggled to earn the respect of non-family employees was repeatedly described with the adage, "Born on third base but thought he hit a triple."[54] Over time, he gave up disputing his image as an arrogant rich kid and acted the part. This deferential treatment can result in feelings of low self-worth and may foster feelings of guilt and shame about being different, and somehow being wrong or undeserving of their inheritance. In fact, wealthy children are sometimes taught to hide their wealth and even lie to peers about it. This compromises their ability to form trusting friendships.

Guilt and shame associated with wealth can even impact relationships among family members within a wealthy family. Wealth transfer decisions motivated by regret, guilt, or shame can later breed resentment, which only worsens the underlying emotional resistance. If not addressed, these feelings can become magnified over several generations and result in dysfunction and conflict. To resolve these feelings, it's helpful to become truly aware of and accept them.

Sometimes, guilt and shame are associated with how wealth is distributed or with perceived favoritism between siblings or one branch of the family and another. Therefore, tensions can arise when one child grows up to be more independently successful than his or her siblings or produces better financial results with an equal inheritance.

Such deeply rooted concerns and feelings can obviously strain relationships. It is not hard to imagine the guilt and resentment in relationships in which one person has significantly greater wealth than the other. When those relationships are strained, it can lead right back to generational trauma, and the cycle continues all over again.

At extremes—whether dealing with children, siblings, parents, friends, or peers—the real "evil" of wealth can be the dysfunction and conflict caused by feelings of regret, guilt, and shame and the resulting triangles.

THE HISTORY OF GUILT AND SHAME

Daniel Sznycer—a social psychologist and assistant professor at the University of Montreal—explains, "Guilt and shame are among the most intense human emotions. No one wants to be constantly reminded of mistakes like cheating on a partner, failing an exam, or letting down a family member. However, despite their discomfort, guilt and shame are not inherently 'bad emotions.'" He continues, "While these feelings can contribute to depression, anxiety, and paranoia, they also encourage us to improve our behavior. When we act in ways we regret, our brain sends signals that push us to change our actions."[55]

His research concluded that guilt and shame serve as an adaptive function that evolved within humans as part of our survival.[56]

Many people, including myself, have always associated guilt and shame as two emotions that are intertwined in a very toxic relationship. However, when we consider the evolution of human emotion, relationships, and societies, guilt and shame have actually served an important role in building community and civilization.

It is thought that the two emotions are designed to protect us from hurting or harming those closest to us and to encourage humans to behave differently to avoid guilt and shame in the future. If you think about it, guilt and shame could be the foundation of building community and relationships.

Throughout human evolution, we have depended on one another to overcome injuries, illnesses, predators, and scarcity. In such a context, a person who consistently harmed others would likely find themselves isolated and unsupported during difficult times, potentially jeopardizing their survival due to a lack of communal care.

If that same individual—driven by feelings of guilt and shame—altered their behavior to become more compassionate and generous, they could take corrective steps and integrate as a valuable member of the community.

Guilt and shame are particularly impactful because they operate at a subconscious level. They relate to both actual and perceived inadequacies and failures. Although they are closely related, it's crucial to distinguish between the two, as they can occur independently.

Guilt is an internal emotion that can exist even if others are unaware of the actions causing it. It often manifests itself without external consequences, prompting only personal feelings of needing to improve, make more effort, or alter future behavior.

Shame, on the other hand, is centered around the fear of someone else finding out what you've done. As a result, it can lead to other damaging actions like dishonesty and inauthenticity. It tends to arise from not wanting to be belittled and unappreciated.

In modern times, guilt and shame can still play an essential role in building community, but we don't face the same challenges we did when these emotions were evolving. Understanding how guilt and shame are associated with inherited wealth can strengthen our communities and families.

EMOTIONAL CONDITIONING

Emotional conditioning occurs when an experience evokes certain emotions, and going forward all related experiences evoke that same emotion. In my experience with my inheritance, as I mentioned before, phrases like "You're so lucky" evoked feelings of guilt in me from a young age. Now, that same phrase in almost any context brings up those same feelings.

It doesn't matter whether you're responsible for the situation or not—like how I have no control over someone else setting up a trust fund for me.

Yet, these repeated experiences of guilt and shame can become harmful when they manifest themselves in negative, self-doubting beliefs. If this happens, feelings of guilt and shame can arise from simple mistakes and include many self-criticisms.

Since children are more likely to internalize guilt, children who experience guilt are also more likely to have excessive guilt in adulthood. They develop a very critical inner voice toward themselves.

While some inheritors, like my sisters, don't know they have a trust fund until early adulthood, others, like me, know from a young age and have plenty of time to build that internal criticism that follows us into adulthood.

In the case of trust funds and inheritance, this kind of conditioning is all tied back to money, wealth, generational wealth, and inheritance.

According to psychologist Jena Field, "Both guilt and shame trigger fear responses in the brain," releasing stress hormones and causing internal anxiety, stress, and tension.[57] While these emotions and reactions also serve a purpose, if they perpetuate throughout daily life—as is often the case with heirs and trust fund recipients—it can have lasting effects on their health and wellness.

IMPACT OF UNADDRESSED EXCESSIVE GUILT AND SHAME

Fear responses are designed to keep us safe. That little tingle on the back of your neck that makes you hyper-aware of your surroundings, or the gut instinct that you should run away, are beneficial. Still, when they kick in, those survival responses rival all other motivations, including healing the wounds of others, reconnecting, making amends, or even learning from past experiences.[58]

Unfortunately, not making amends or reparations can subconsciously fuel our own negative feelings toward ourselves. It creates a shame cycle of destructive behaviors, because when we're locked in that survival state we can't override it to change our behaviors or actions.[59]

It can also result in more self-destructive behaviors like excessive drinking, substance abuse, not caring about financial security, and impulse spending. These behaviors stem from wanting to block out, numb, or ignore feelings of shame.[60]

When I look back on my impulsive spending habits and some of the bad choices I made with money, I can relate them to my own detachment from my money, which was almost a defense mechanism I developed to block out the guilt and shame I felt for having it.

Shame and guilt that are unaddressed and perpetuated can lead to anxiety, depression, resentment, anger issues, and a lot of self-destructive behaviors.[61] At the beginning of the chapter, I mentioned how guilt and shame can be suddenly woven into everyday life for inheritors. That is the perfect storm for being stuck in a state of survival and unable to break out of guilt or shame, continuing the cycle to more destructive tendencies.

Fortunately, it is possible to release guilt and shame and build a healthier relationship with your money, inheritance, and yourself.

LEAVE YOUR BURDENS BEHIND

Not everyone who inherits wealth experiences guilt and shame. I don't want anyone to think that they should feel guilt or shame if they don't, or, conversely, that if they feel it, they are alone.

The first step to releasing guilt and shame is to become aware of these feelings, acknowledge that they exist, and then look for their source.

A lot of times, wealth, guilt, and shame are sourced from someone else's perceptions and feelings toward you and your circumstances. The feelings are imposed until you are conditioned to have them.

Recognize that you cannot control whether a sibling feels that your parents gave you more love or support. Or that a high school friend resented the new car you were given at age 16. Or that your wealthy in-laws question your motives in marrying their child. Of course, you also can't control the fact that the latest box office hit unfairly stereotypes the wealthy as dishonest or ruthless. Adopting others' feelings that conflict with your own sense of self may only encourage those who want to shift their feelings onto you.

Society is very focused on material wealth as a measuring stick. The reality of being wealthy is that others may feel the need to make you think that you are "wrong" in order to deflect their own feelings of inadequacy and failure. We all naturally take on some of these transferred feelings—it's only human to do so. But if you can increase your awareness of any feelings of regret, guilt, or shame linked to your wealth, you can reduce the outside influences over your own sense of self-worth and hope. Resist popular perceptions.

One of the ways I've seen people succumb to the guilt and shame of societal expectations is by giving to philanthropy out of pure guilt and pressure from societal expectations. This is not a productive way to give back and use your resources—it will only result in a cycle of guilt. Giving because of guilt and the residual feelings of not being aligned with that gift will cause more guilt and regret. While giving your money, time, resources, etc. can be very rewarding, it should come from the desire to give back and help others, not from feeling guilty about what you have.

Refuse to accept or fall victim to stereotypes. You might see your wealth in a healthier perspective, as something you can be proud to have created through your own honest efforts or received by legitimate inheritance or other good fortune.

Despite the views of others around you or prevailing media images, you can see your wealth as a wonderful blessing, just like good health, good looks, athletic ability, or above-average intelligence. Self-acceptance will enhance your ability to use your wealth in ways that honor yourself and your values and more freely benefit others. One of the first actions I took when I started becoming aware of these patterns and feelings was to manage my money in a way that felt comfortable to me.

It's why I bought a house, as I mentioned in chapter one, because the money became a blessing and a means for me to support myself through rental income while I took a healing journey. It wasn't easy to separate myself from my money or the guilt and shame associated with it, but once I started, it gave me a whole new feeling of accomplishment and abundance.

STEPS FOR OVERCOMING GUILT AND SHAME

Guilt and shame are related emotions, but they have distinct differences in their underlying causes and emotional responses:

- Guilt: Guilt is primarily a response to a specific behavior or action. It arises when you believe you have done something wrong or violated your own moral or ethical code.
  - It often involves focusing on the behavior itself and feeling responsible for its consequences.
  - Guilt can be a motivating emotion, prompting you to make amends, change your behavior, or take responsibility for your actions.
  - It is considered a healthy emotion when it helps guide you toward more ethical and considerate behavior.

- Shame: Shame, on the other hand, is a more profound and pervasive emotion. It is not solely tied to a particular action but rather to your sense of self or identity.
  - Shame involves feeling fundamentally flawed, inadequate, or unworthy. It often stems from negative self-beliefs and can result from internalizing criticism or negative messages from others.
  - Unlike guilt, shame is not typically a motivating emotion for positive change. Instead, it often leads to withdrawal, isolation, and a deep sense of worthlessness.
  - Shame can be highly detrimental to one's self-esteem and mental well-being and is considered an unhealthy emotion when it becomes chronic and overwhelming.

In summary, guilt is related to feeling bad about a specific behavior or action and is focused on the action itself. On the other hand, shame is a more generalized feeling of being inherently flawed or unworthy. Understanding the distinction between the two emotions can help address and manage them effectively. Guilt can lead to constructive changes, while shame often requires extensive work on self-esteem and self-compassion.

Overcoming guilt and shame can be a challenging process, but it's essential for your emotional well-being and personal growth. It is a gradual process, and it may take time. Seek support from friends, family, or a therapist if you find it challenging to manage your feelings of guilt on your own. Additionally, practicing mindfulness and forgiveness can be helpful in the journey to overcoming guilt and finding emotional peace.

Even now, it still creeps up on me sometimes. But I know I've come a long way compared to where I was before I started my healing journey.

Steps for inheritors to overcome guilt and shame:

- Self-awareness and acknowledgment: Start by recognizing and acknowledging your feelings of guilt and shame. Understand that these emotions are common among inheritors and that they may be rooted in various factors, including family dynamics, societal expectations, or personal values.
- Reflect on your values and beliefs: Take the time to clarify your own values and beliefs regarding wealth, privilege, and responsibility. Consider what you genuinely believe about your financial situation and how it aligns with your ethics.
- Seek professional guidance: Consulting with a therapist, counselor, coach, or financial advisor who specializes in issues related to wealth and inheritance can be helpful. They can provide valuable insights and strategies for managing guilt and shame effectively.

- Establish boundaries and goals: Determine how you want to use your wealth or trust fund in alignment with your values and goals. Setting clear boundaries and establishing a plan for your financial resources can help reduce feelings of guilt and give you a sense of purpose.
- Engage in philanthropy and giving: Many inheritors find that giving back to their communities or donating to causes they care about can be powerful ways to alleviate guilt and shame. Develop a philanthropic strategy that allows you to use your resources for a positive impact.
- Educate yourself: Learn about wealth inequality, privilege, and social justice issues. Understanding the broader context of wealth and its impact on society can help you gain perspective on your own situation and find ways to make a difference.
- Foster open communication: Engage in open and honest discussions with family members and loved ones about your feelings and desire to navigate your financial situation responsibly. Family support and understanding can be crucial in addressing guilt and shame.
- Practice self-compassion: Be kind and patient as you work through these emotions. Remember that your feelings are valid, and seeking help and guidance in managing them is okay.
- Connect with like-minded individuals: Join support groups or communities of individuals who share similar financial backgrounds and experiences. Sharing experiences and insights with others who understand your situation can be comforting and beneficial.

Overcoming guilt and shame related to trust funds or inherited wealth is a personal and ongoing process. It requires self-reflection, education, and a commitment to aligning your financial resources with your values and goals. It's essential to seek professional support and surround yourself with a supportive network of friends and family who can help you navigate this journey.

Since I started talking about these feelings with my siblings and reaching out to others, I've learned I'm not alone. Sharing with others has given me new perspectives on the complexities of guilt and shame as they relate to inherited wealth.

It is entirely possible to release these feelings and start feeling good about yourself, your position in life, and the blessing of abundance you've received.

For more customized tools and resources on
Guilt and Shame, visit trustyourtrustfund.com.

CHAPTER 5

THE POWER OF PURPOSE AND FULFILLMENT

There have been times in my life when I felt aimless, wandering, and directionless. I know my father went through periods of time like that, too. When we're not sure where we're going or what we want to do, we lack purpose. That directionless feeling can contribute to emptiness and a lack of fulfillment.

While lacking purpose and fulfillment isn't exclusive to inheritors or affluent families, I've discovered it is a common deficiency among those surrounded by substantial wealth.

MY JOURNEY WITH PURPOSE

Growing up, I had an undeniable love and passion for horses. It was something I was involved with every day and always looked forward to.

Since I was a little kid, I have been obsessed with horses and naturally good with them. My dad's first wife always had horses, and one of my sisters was always a great rider. This was my introduction to horses.

Shortly after my father passed, they had an extra horse, Shada, and my sisters' mom decided to gift her to me. I'd ridden a lot before, but I had never had a horse of my own. I decided that instead of keeping her at the ranch, I wanted to be able to ride every day, so I boarded Shada at the local fairgrounds.

Horses are a lot of work—I had to go to the fairgrounds every day before school to feed her and after school to clean out her stall, brush her, and ride her.

This gave me a regular routine. She taught me consistency and responsibility and fueled my passion for horses and riding. I learned a lot and felt very fulfilled.

It was all girls at the barn with their horses, and they were into barrel racing. Naturally, I befriended them and started getting into barrel racing and other rodeo events. Eventually, I outgrew Shada. She was a great starter horse, but she wasn't the right fit at the level I wanted to compete. So, I got Playboy, my second horse. He was younger and a quick learner.

It didn't take long for Playboy to whip around barrels and poles. He was so athletic. I didn't want to run barrels with him, but he was a natural. I started competing with him, and he was amazing, winning ribbons, money, and notoriety. Everyone was surprised to find out I was his only rider and trainer.

He was such a natural with barrels that I let some of my girlfriends from the barn compete with him in bigger rodeos. He was winning everything, so we brought him to a prominent Vegas rodeo. A friend rode him and won.

As I was wrapping up high school and getting ready to leave Colorado, I realized I couldn't keep Playboy. I needed to sell him to someone who

Running barrels on Playboy.

would keep competing with him and letting him do what he loved. It was an exciting time for me because he was valued at six or seven times the amount I paid for him. It was also a little sad because I loved him, and it broke my heart to think he'd have another rider soon.

Then, I got a call while I was at work. It was seven in the morning, and my sister's stepdad, was on the phone. He is like a second father to me and my brother, though it was odd for him to call me so early.

He told me that Playboy got out of the barn in the middle of the night. He ran into the road and was hit by a car.

I was devastated. Playboy had so much potential in his competing career. He was just starting out. I'd trained him and ridden him. He was my purpose during those years. I was sad that he never reached his full potential as a champion and devastated that he was gone from the world. At the same time, I felt a strange sense of peace, knowing that he would always be my horse and only my horse. He was meant to be just mine.

Playboy's passing was a sudden end to my childhood equine career. I was still on track to leave Colorado and didn't know where life would take me. Since then, I have ridden and helped out at the ranch. I still maintain my innate talent with horses, and my love and connection to them hasn't waned. While it isn't my current focus, one of my goals is to have a horse ranch one day where I can continue my dream of competing. When I look back on that time, such a strong sense of purpose led to fulfillment. Purpose and fulfillment are closely related concepts, but they refer to different aspects of human experience.

Purpose relates to the reason or intention behind one's actions, existence, or goals. It's about having a sense of direction or meaning in life, understanding why you do what you do, and feeling connected to something larger than yourself. Purpose often involves identifying values, passions, and long-term objectives. It gives life direction and can serve as a guiding principle for decision-making and goal setting.

On the other hand, fulfillment refers to a sense of satisfaction, contentment, or completeness derived from achieving or pursuing one's purpose, goals, or desires. It's feeling deeply gratified and emotionally satisfied with one's life, accomplishments, relationships, or experiences. Fulfillment often arises when individuals align their actions and behaviors with their values and purpose, leading to a sense of inner peace, joy, and meaning.

Purpose provides the overarching reason or direction in life, while fulfillment is the emotional and psychological reward gained from living in alignment with that purpose.

In my own experience, my purpose has changed throughout different stages of my life. In my adolescence, my purpose centered around my equine career. Now, it is centered around helping people—especially those with inherited wealth.

THE POWER OF PURPOSE

I've found that many people feel their purpose is a big, daunting idea. I've noticed that it has revealed itself organically when I wasn't searching for my purpose. But when I was searching for purpose, it led me down the wrong path and felt daunting. I believe that it is when we try new and different things that purpose comes to the surface and reveals itself.

Purpose is all about asking *why*. Why are you doing what you're doing? What's driving you to achieve? What is it you want to achieve?

I've worked with many coaches and clients, and a common theme when working with purpose is that there are many misconceptions about purpose. When asked, "Why do you want to start a business?" the most common answer is, "To make money."

Money isn't a purpose—it's a result. It is important to differentiate the two because many people chase results instead of their purpose. But when you get deeper into the *why*, it helps you uncover a lot about yourself, your desires, and consequently how to allocate your resources and focus your energy.

In terms of inheritance, this could include what to use your inheritance for, or it could help you establish your own identity apart from your money and your family legacy.

Purpose isn't a streamlined thing. It is important to have purpose in all the areas of your life: career, relationships, health, physical, spiritual, emotional, financial, social, personal growth, etc. This also brings up the concept of internal versus external purpose. External and internal purposes refer to the sources from which one derives their sense of direction, meaning, and fulfillment. External purpose is derived from factors outside of oneself, such as societal expectations, cultural norms, or external goals imposed by others.

It may involve fulfilling family obligations, meeting societal standards of success, or adhering to professional expectations. External purposes are often influenced by external pressures, societal norms, or expectations from others, and they may not always align with one's personal values or desires. Many inheritors struggle with their external purpose because of family values and expectations, societal stigmas, and not being given the space to discover their internal purpose.

Internal purpose, on the other hand, comes from within oneself. Personal values, passions, interests, and intrinsic motivations drive it. Internal purpose is about discovering and pursuing what truly matters to you, regardless of external pressures or expectations. It involves listening to your inner voice, following your intuition, and aligning your actions with your authentic self. Internal purpose often leads to a deeper sense of fulfillment and satisfaction because it stems from genuine self-awareness and alignment with one's core values and beliefs.

While external purposes may provide direction and structure in certain contexts, internal purposes tend to be more enduring and personally fulfilling because they are rooted in individual authenticity and intrinsic motivation.

Striking a balance between external and internal purposes can lead to a more meaningful and fulfilling life.

The relationship between purpose and fulfillment can vary from person to person and situation to situation. For some individuals, discovering their purpose may lead to a greater sense of fulfillment, while for others, fulfillment may precede the discovery of purpose. Here are a few scenarios to illustrate the different ways purpose and fulfillment may interact:

- Purpose leads to fulfillment: Some people find that identifying and pursuing their purpose in life brings them a deep sense of fulfillment. When they have clarity about their values, passions, and goals, and they actively work toward living in alignment with their purpose, they experience a greater sense of satisfaction, meaning, and joy.

- Fulfillment leads to purpose: In other cases, individuals may first experience fulfillment through engaging in activities, relationships, or experiences that bring them joy and satisfaction. These experiences may give them insights into what truly matters to them and help them develop a clearer sense of purpose over time.

- Iterative process: Discovering purpose and experiencing fulfillment can be an iterative process that unfolds over time. As individuals explore different paths, try new experiences, and engage in self-reflection, they may refine their understanding of their purpose and what brings them fulfillment. Each step toward living authentically and aligning with their values can lead to greater fulfillment and a deeper sense of purpose.

- Simultaneous discovery: For some people, the discovery of purpose and the experience of fulfillment may occur simultaneously or in close succession. They may have a clear sense of purpose that resonates deeply with them, and as they begin to pursue it they find fulfillment in the process of living in alignment with their purpose.

My dad is an excellent example from my life because I don't think he ever found his purpose or fulfillment. He had a degree in physical education but never did anything with it. He always talked about the idea of becoming a PE teacher, and since his passing it's something that my family has talked about frequently. I bring this up again because this is a perfect example of a career that would have brought him so much purpose and fulfillment.

Maybe the external expectations caused him not to move forward with a career in this space. Some wealthy families look at certain career paths like being a teacher as being "beneath" them. I don't think that's how my father felt, but I know of others who have felt unable to pursue their passions because it would disparage the upscale image some families of means like to project.

Based on the kind of guy my dad was, he would have been the best PE teacher and every student's favorite. Plus, the impact and value he would have provided to countless students would have brought a sense of fulfillment that would've changed his life. Don't get me wrong—he had external purposes, like me and my siblings and his family. They weren't enough to keep him on track, though. External purposes can be very powerful, but the most empowering and satisfying purpose comes from within. If my dad had focused on his internal purpose in life, he would still be here and living his best life.

Both purpose and fulfillment hold immense power in shaping our lives and experiences. Purpose provides us with direction, guiding our decisions and actions toward meaningful goals and aspirations. It gives our lives clarity, meaning, and a sense of significance. When we're aligned with our purpose, we feel a deep sense of fulfillment, satisfaction, and inner peace.

Fulfillment, however, represents the culmination of living in alignment with our purpose—the profound sense of contentment, happiness, and completeness we experience when we engage in activities, relationships, and endeavors that resonates deeply with our values and passions. Fulfillment enriches every aspect of our lives, from our well-being and resilience to our relationships and sense of purpose.

Together, purpose and fulfillment empower us to live with intention, meaning, and joy.

A GUIDING LIGHT

Purpose is often seen as a guiding light that helps us find fulfillment and meaning in life. But it's not as simple as it might seem from the motivational posters, speeches, and daily affirmations. Research spanning more than 30 years shows that purpose is a bit more complicated but also hopeful.[62]

Instead of thinking of purpose as one thing we must discover, studies suggest that it can be found in different parts of our lives. It's not a fixed destination—we don't just stumble upon it. Instead, it's something we develop over time by thinking about what's important to us and taking intentional actions. Like happiness, purpose is more of a journey than a final goal.

Research has shown that having purpose reduces stress and can guide you toward channeling challenges for growth and learning. The researchers concluded that having a purposeful life fueled hope and optimism. It also contributed to better health and longevity. When looking at older people, there was a physical correlation between having more purpose and less functional decline.[63]

People with purpose didn't experience as much weakening of their musculature, had less cognitive and memory impairment, and even a lower risk of Alzheimer's disease. Overall, people with more purpose lead healthier lives and make healthier choices like exercise, better nutrition, and preventative behaviors like cancer screenings and being mindful of their cholesterol.[64]

Additionally, studies have posited that a purpose-driven life leads to healthier aging and reduces mortality risk. One study, which was conducted over a period of 14 years, followed purposeful individuals and their counterparts. Even when accounting for other factors that could inhibit psychological well-being, it was concluded that purposeful people had a wide buffer against mortality risks such as heart attack, high cholesterol, and even cancer.[65]

Finding and nurturing our purpose is something we can do at any age, as long as we're willing to think about our values, dreams, and the kind of person we want to be. Purpose isn't something we figure out once and then forget about—it's something we keep working on throughout our lives. By revisiting and updating our sense of purpose as we go through different stages of life, we can live more fulfilling and meaningful lives.

Certified Financial Planner Myra Salzer with the Wealth Conservatory said, "People who've earned [their money] have a different relationship with their wealth than those to whom it's been given....If you haven't earned it through your own efforts, there's a sense of scarcity around it....If you've earned it, you're quite a bit more capable of taking risks, knowing you can always earn it again....We have a strong work ethic in this country. We admire the person who's made it, not the person who's just gotten it. We define ourselves by what we do for a living. It's important that people have work that feels purposeful and feels like they're contributing to the community. It can be paid work, volunteer work, or work in a family business or foundation."[66]

Since many inheritors are born into families with strong values and expectations, they aren't always encouraged to discover their own values or purpose. As a result, they end up like my dad and many others—aimless and directionless.

An article for the *Journal of Applied Developmental Psychology* in 2010 looked at whether or not purpose and one's life goals could predict both short and long-term personal well-being. The study followed over 400 college undergraduates who were tested at graduation and then again 13 years later. The study found that those who maintained a sense of purpose into their middle adulthood had "greater generativity, personal growth, and integrity," especially those who were prosocial and beyond self-goals. Engaging in prosocial goals had more impact than focusing on other kinds of goals.[67]

Purpose is inherently subjective. It is deeply personal and varies from individual to individual based on their values, beliefs, experiences, and aspirations. What gives one person a sense of purpose may differ entirely from what motivates or fulfills another person. Nowadays, it seems everyone is talking about purpose and the journey to discover your purpose, which is also subjective.

Unfortunately, I've seen many inheritors and wealthy families that hold their core family values above all else. People aren't allowed to have that subjective individuality that would lead them to their own purpose outside what their families expect or want.

For those of us who receive inheritances, sometimes money can feel like a reason to ignore our own personal development in favor of family values because of the great gift of wealth. The inheritance becomes an invisible, gilded cage, causing us to feel indebted to those family beliefs, expectations, and values.

DISCOVERING YOUR PURPOSE

Discovering your purpose is a deeply personal journey that often involves self-reflection, exploration, and experimentation.

Here are some ways you can begin to uncover your purpose:

- Reflect on your passions and interests: Consider the activities, topics, or causes that you feel most drawn to or enthusiastic about. For me, it was horses when I was younger—an easy answer because

I put so much time into it. The answer might not be as easy for some of us to pinpoint. Think about those times when you've felt most alive or engaged, and identify common themes or patterns.

- Assess your strengths and skills: Take inventory of your talents, strengths, and skills. Consider the things that come naturally to you or that you excel at. Your purpose may align with leveraging these abilities to positively impact or contribute to something meaningful.

- Clarify your values and beliefs: Reflect on what matters most to you in life. Identify your core values, beliefs, and principles. Your purpose is often closely tied to living in alignment with these values and making choices that honor them.

- Explore different experiences and opportunities: Be open to trying new things and stepping outside your comfort zone. Explore different roles, activities, and environments to better understand what resonates with you and where you feel most fulfilled.

- Seek inspiration from others: Learn from the experiences and wisdom of others who have found their purpose. Read books, listen to podcasts, attend workshops, or engage with mentors who can offer insights and guidance.

- Pay attention to feedback and intuition: Listen to the feedback you receive from others about your strengths, talents, and impact. Also, listen to your intuition and inner voice. Trust your instincts and pay attention to the activities or opportunities that energize and inspire you.

- Reflect on past experiences: Look back on significant moments or experiences that have shaped who you are today. Consider how these experiences have influenced your values, interests, and aspirations and how they might inform your sense of purpose.

- Set meaningful goals: Define specific, meaningful goals that align with your passions, values, and strengths. Working toward these goals can provide clarity and direction and help uncover aspects of your purpose.

- Practice mindfulness and self-awareness: Cultivate mindfulness and self-awareness through meditation, journaling, or therapy. These practices can help you better understand yourself, your motivations, and your purpose.
- Give back and make a difference: Engage in activities or volunteer work that allow you to make a positive impact and contribute to something larger than yourself. Serving others and making a difference can provide a sense of purpose and fulfillment.

PURPOSE EVOLVES

My equine career stopped being my central purpose when I turned 18 and left Colorado to start my adult life. Although my deep passion and purpose were centered around my horses when I was growing up, I had other desires to explore the world and seek what else was out there for me. I also trusted that I would one day have horses again and that my many evolving purposes would align. I didn't always know my purpose, and sometimes I felt like I was "between purposes" as I moved through the different phases of my life. After going through a lot of healing, if I felt lost or directionless I'd look at myself and see what aligned best with my purpose at that point in my life.

Discovering your purpose is an ongoing process that evolves over time. Be patient with yourself, stay curious, and remain open to new possibilities. Trust that you'll gradually uncover a deeper sense of purpose and meaning in your life by taking intentional steps toward self-discovery.

A 2019 research paper published by *Applied Developmental Science* suggests that the development of purpose in childhood and young adulthood has an important impact on one's overall development. During their research, they found that those who were purposeful measured higher in areas of positive adaptation and development. This study looked at purpose as it developed from childhood into adulthood and later in life.[68]

When we live with purpose and experience fulfillment, we unlock our full potential and positively impact the world. Purpose and fulfillment fuel our creativity, productivity, and effectiveness, enabling us to approach challenges with resilience, innovation, and resourcefulness. They deepen our connections with ourselves and others, fostering greater self-awareness, authenticity, and empathy.

This is why many inheritors end up in the same ruts and the same stigmatized situations. They never have the chance to unlock their full potential. Sometimes, it's because their path has been chosen for them. Other times it's because what they are drawn to doesn't align with the family image or values. Maybe they were never encouraged to pursue their passions.

It's also why I think many inheritors struggle with interpersonal relationships. It's hard to truly care about someone and be there for them, or accept affection and support in return, if we don't know ourselves or don't love ourselves. And when we don't know our purpose, it is easy to lack self-love.

The power of purpose and fulfillment lies in our ability to enrich every aspect of our lives, from our well-being and resilience to our relationships and sense of meaning. By cultivating purpose and seeking fulfillment, we can lead more meaningful, joyful, and fulfilling lives, creating a positive impact for ourselves and those around us.

When I decided to write this book, I had recently found a new purpose. Previously, coaching had been my main purpose. I had come to this purpose when I took action and started trying new and different things. When I first got into coaching, I was focused on coaching men on their identity and sexuality. After struggling with these issues myself in my childhood and the positive effects coming out had on my life, I aimed to help other men do the same. I enjoyed the work, but I realized over time that it wasn't the niche I was genuinely called to serve.

In one of my alternative therapy sessions, I had the insight to write a book about trust funds. As I was talking to one of my friends, who's also a mentor in business, I mentioned the trust fund book. She threw her hands up, widened her eyes, and said, "This is genius! This is it." She explained how my new insight provided a specific problem with a specific client and that there wasn't anyone offering that kind of service or support.

I immediately saw the need and went out to fill that gap. Choosing this course challenged me to the root of my being, and the fear of the unknown has guided me forward.

Since going out and serving this niche, I have found a more profound sense of purpose and fulfillment in my career. Even though the previous niche and client base were meaningful and close to home, this felt even closer and more meaningful. Given that this has affected my dad, my uncle, my siblings, and so many others so intensely, it truly is a dream to be helping people just like them.

I transitioned away from the coaching I had been doing before because another purpose had called to me. My purpose now is to empower trust funders and inheritors to discover their unique paths to purpose, fulfillment, and resource optimization, enabling them to make a transformative impact on the world. I'm guided by my deep commitment to catalyzing positive change, and my mission is to equip individuals with the tools, insights, and support they need to leverage their resources for meaningful and sustainable contributions to society.

Driven by a profound "big why," I am dedicated to unlocking the potential of those with the means to effect significant change, recognizing the immense power and responsibility inherent in their resources. By facilitating introspection, clarity, and strategic action, I aim to inspire trust funders and inheritors to harness their wealth and influence for the betterment of humanity and the planet.

With a focus on facilitating purpose-driven decision-making, cultivating fulfillment, and optimizing resource allocation, I aspire to create a ripple effect of positive impact that extends far beyond individual lives. Through personalized coaching, mentorship, and guidance, I strive to empower my clients to align their actions with their values, amplify their impact, and leave a lasting legacy of meaningful change.

Pursuing this purpose, I have committed to continuous growth, learning, and evolution, recognizing that the journey toward transformative impact is ongoing and iterative. Rooted in authenticity, integrity, and empathy, I can foster a supportive and collaborative environment where trust funders and inheritors feel empowered to explore, discover, and actualize their highest aspirations for themselves and the world.

Knowing my purpose has brought me so many opportunities and helped me learn more about myself and what it means to be part of a family with generational wealth. I am no longer aimlessly wandering and questioning, "Why me? What is this all for?" I've been able to step away from relying on inherited wealth for basic needs and create the life and business I desire. I can now focus my inheritance on more productive ways of giving back, growing it, and preserving it for future generations.

I used to shop uncontrollably, trying to fill a void I didn't understand. I recklessly spent money because I didn't understand the value of a dollar and felt no attachment to it. Now, I'm moving forward consciously, with purpose. There is no longer any void that needs to be filled.

For more customized tools and resources on Purpose
and Fulfillment, visit trustyourtrustfund.com.

CHAPTER 6
FINANCIAL LITERACY AND MANAGEMENT

While my parents were married, my mother was blessed with the same financial stability and wealth that came with being part of a wealthy family. For several years, she experienced that abundance. However, she didn't learn how to manage funds or think about money in a sustainable way.

After they divorced, my mom received a settlement. During the divorce process, they decided to sell our childhood home. That house carried a $600 mortgage and very reasonable property taxes.

I'm not sure why the decision was made to sell the house, but the cost was low, and my mother could have easily managed it on her own. It provided us with some stability.

Once the house was sold, we bounced around between fourteen rental houses that cost a minimum of $1,500 monthly. There was no longer stability, and the payments were much higher than my mom could afford. The higher cost of living, and my mom sticking to her old spending habits, caused her to completely drain the settlement funds when it could have set her up nicely.

Even though she started working right after the divorce, it wasn't enough. She didn't have the knowledge or financial literacy to use her resources advantageously.

She could have used settlement money as a down payment on a new house to lower our family's cost of living and provide more stability. We lived in Colorado, and at the time the housing market could have easily allowed her to purchase an affordable house that would have increased tremendously in value.

Without a plan or an understanding of finances, she depleted her liquid assets and lost an opportunity.

DON'T LET YOUR MONEY CONTROL YOU

Even though my mom wasn't born into wealth like my dad, she did grow up in privileged and abundant circumstances. Her father always made good money and lived in an affluent community. I think part of her lack of knowledge about money comes from her father taking care of her for the majority of her adolescence. Then she met my father, who took the reins.

One of my favorite photos of my parents.

It always worked out for her. She is an "in-the-moment" person and never stressed about the future until she had to. She is also the most generous person I've ever met. She was never stingy with money and always gave us incredible gifts, trips, memories, and the best childhood she could. She was generous with everyone and never felt scarcity around the money she did have.

When she got her divorce settlement, like many people who suddenly acquire a large sum of money, she didn't have the support or resources to manage it effectively. This entire experience shaped who she is today.

Now, she is 100% independent and killing it in business. She is making more money than she thought possible for herself and has learned from her financial mishaps to create the future she desires. She is highly meticulous, on top of her finances, and always says she would never let herself get back to the places she had been financially before.

Ultimately, this was all necessary for her evolution and personal growth. I'm extremely proud of her.

It can happen with people who grow up in wealthy families once they get access to their trust funds, too. I've seen it with members of my own family who drain their accounts and then rely on other family members to support them.

If my mother had created the right infrastructure to manage that money, she could have set herself up to live comfortably and not have to work so hard.

On the flip side, there are people in my family who have used their trust funds more effectively. One of my sisters decided to invest in her husband's company. It was a risk, but she trusted him and calculated the reward payout before making a decision. Once his company got up and running, it generated more cash flow than her trust fund ever had. Her husband has the drive and motivation to grow and scale the company.

Not only has it grown her net worth and initial investment, but it has given her the freedom to be a stay-at-home mom and raise her four children.

I spoke to another inheritor, Nadia, and it resonated with her because she grew up in a similar situation. Her inheritance came from her father's side, but her parents were divorced, and she was raised by her mother, who didn't have a trust fund or wealth to fall back on.[69]

Nadia's family wealth came from her grandmother's parents, who were on her father's side. They were one of the wealthiest families in Chicago at the time. She didn't know exactly where her family's wealth came from, but she knew that they worked with important people in politics. She recalled that they were in the printing business when the government transitioned to printing money. She was the fifth generation of inheritance and knew that all her cousins had trust funds.

As Nadia says, when you have the freedom to use so much money, it can take on a life of its own. It can happen frequently with inheritors. But when the money is out of your hands, there's more control over how it's used.

Like my sisters, she found out about her trust fund when she was between 16 and 18. The deal was that as long as Nadia was in college, her trust would pay for college and her bills. She sent her trustee her list of expenses every month, and then her trustee gave her the money for it from her trust.

For Nadia, to get access to funds in her trust before she was 25 was contingent on her being in college. She'd still get access to the trust at 25, regardless. Having some educational provision isn't uncommon with trust funds—whether the money needs to be used for education or can't be accessed unless, or until, the recipient is in college or has graduated.

Sometimes, these contingencies force inheritors into educational programs and situations they otherwise wouldn't choose in the face of giving up their inheritance. It can be a weighty decision for young adults in their late teens or early 20s.

Nadia says that it was a provision in her trust because her family wanted everyone to get an education. She said that it motivated her to go to college. She desired to go beforehand, but the trust fund contingency helped.

Growing up, she remembers that money was an ongoing issue between her parents. They fought a lot about money, and it eventually tore them apart. Her dad never paid her mom any child support when they split, and he was rarely around. He'd make up excuses about not paying on time.

She's seen multiple examples in her family of people who have benefitted from different investments—especially real estate. But not everyone in her family was a beacon of inspiration for generosity, investing, and success. Her uncle, for instance, was a little rebellious and struggled with drugs and alcohol. As a result, his mother supported him.

Nadia looks back on things with an interesting perspective. She says that because she was able to travel and do what she loved, now she won't settle for something that takes her away from her passion. She knows she can't just sit at a nine-to-five job. Those experiences motivated her to make a successful, profitable career out of something she loves.

For her, it's been a journey that's forced her to change her relationship, mindset, and emotions about money.

Unlike some, she didn't fall into partying or unhealthy habits. She did a lot with her time and money but didn't have a plan to rebuild what she was spending. She did say that during the last few months when she had some money and was watching it dwindle, she was very anxious and kept wondering what she would do.

If you are inheriting your assets or have a trust fund coming your way, it is important to gain a reasonable understanding of financial literacy and management. Not only will this help you maintain and grow your wealth, but it can also combat a lot of the more detrimental mental health burdens that come with inheriting.

As I started to learn more about my trust, the investments, and how it all worked, I was able to take control of my life and my financial situation. I was ruling the money instead of the other way around. This is a way to immediately feel more empowered and in control of your finances and future.

HAVING MONEY DOESN'T EQUAL FINANCIAL LITERACY

Trust funders and inheritors face unique financial circumstances, often managing significant wealth passed down through generations. The importance of financial literacy and management must be balanced. Understanding financial concepts and strategies is crucial for navigating the complexities of inherited wealth, including various assets like stocks, bonds, real estate, and business interests. Without a solid grasp of financial principles, trust funders and inheritors may struggle to make informed decisions about preserving and growing their wealth, potentially exposing themselves to unnecessary risks and missing opportunities.

Nadia's brother, while she didn't know every detail or what he did with his money, knew that he didn't have many investments—no real estate and maybe some minor crypto investments. Her brother thinks that he got his trust too early. He says he was too young and didn't know what he wanted.

She says she's often felt the same way, like, "Oh, my God, I have all this money, and I have no fucking clue what I'm going to do with it."

When she got her money and was living in Portugal, she married a guy who worked for his parents' company. They were also living in his parents' house at the time and not paying rent. They were pretty well off, but Nadia's husband was still trying to make it and figure out what he wanted to do. In the meantime, they traveled a lot.

When the money came in, Nadia started to pay for everything. The money from her trust allowed her to teach yoga full-time and start making jewelry, but she never had to scale the company. Beforehand, she couldn't live off a yoga teacher's salary.

At the same time, she was watching money fly out of her account for bills, and it caused a lot of stress and anxiety because it was leaving and not being made up. Even now, she says that even though she's making money, she still has anxiety when she spends money on things.

The way Nadia put it was, if you had $500 in your account, it's like, "Oh yeah!" But you're not going to beat yourself up for losing that. It's fairly easy to make up again. When you have $5 million in your account, you're going to be really nervous about losing it. If you do lose it, you'll spend the rest of your life beating yourself up if you don't have your stuff together.

Nadia received her trust fund at the age of 25. By 29, she had spent it all. When Nadia turned 25 and was entitled to her money, she talked to her trust advisor, and within a week, all the money was transferred to her account. She said it was so easy to see all that money show up, and then super stressful to watch it dwindle.

As I saw with some of my family members, one of the biggest obstacles they faced was a lack of financial education. Since they grew up surrounded by wealth and had inherited wealth to rely on, they never learned to respect or manage money.

I had the unique perspective of living with my mom, who struggled financially, and it helped me see both sides.

Nadia says that what she's seen and experienced with her family and their wealth has inspired her to create wealth again. She doesn't have kids, and one of the reasons she's held off is that she wants them to be well set up. She saw her mom struggle and doesn't want that for her kids.

Managing money goes beyond just knowing what's in your account and what you're spending it on. It's knowing how to make the best financial decisions for your situation, using basic tools like budgeting, and utilizing investments with proper risk analysis.

People who are born into wealth and then inherit trust funds aren't always taught proper financial management. It's often overlooked because it is easy to forget that when you don't have to worry about things like paying bills, you can forget where the money comes from and that it's finite.

Financial literacy refers to the knowledge and understanding of financial concepts, tools, and strategies that individuals need in order to make informed and effective financial decisions. It encompasses various aspects of personal finance, including budgeting, saving, investing, borrowing, and managing debt.

Financially literate individuals are equipped to navigate financial challenges, plan for the future, and confidently achieve their financial goals. They understand concepts such as interest rates, inflation, risk diversification, and taxation, enabling them to make sound financial decisions that contribute to their overall financial well-being.

Financial literacy empowers individuals to take control of their finances, build wealth, and secure their financial futures.

When a trust fund is set up, a lot of the technical part is taken care of. The financial managers who manage trusts are often responsible for taxes, managing stock market investments, etc. Financial managers are paid a decent amount of money to know how to make the best moves.

You don't need to be a seasoned financial manager to understand the terms, know where your money is going, and learn how to make informed decisions about your account and wealth that will benefit you.

It can be easier to leave all that in someone else's hands. If you want to take control of your financial future and ensure that you're managing your trust fund effectively, you should get familiar with the basic terms and look into what you can do yourself. If you are interested in taking that deep dive, there are books and professionals who can help you with financial literacy and managing your wealth. The point of this chapter is not to teach you financial literacy but to outline its importance and benefits for inheritors.

THE FIVE KEY COMPONENTS OF FINANCIAL LITERACY AND WEALTH MANAGEMENT

I've spoken to inheritors who were overwhelmed by the idea of managing such a large sum of money. It can be daunting to try to figure out how best to allocate funds for different endeavors, such as investment opportunities.

The fundamentals of financial management are the same whether you're managing a minimum-wage paycheck or a substantial trust fund. Knowing these fundamentals puts you in a much better position to make informed decisions about your finances. These five components can be scaled for any amount of money.

1. Budgeting

Budgeting involves creating a plan for how to spend and save your money. It starts with understanding your income and expenses. This includes identifying sources of income, such as salaries, wages, or any other sources of revenue, and categorizing expenses into essential or needed items, and non-essential or desired items. By setting limits on spending and prioritizing financial goals, individuals can effectively manage their finances and ensure they're living within their means. Budgeting helps to track where money is going, identify areas where spending can be reduced, and allocate funds toward savings and investments for future goals.

The great thing about budgets is that they are a bit subjective. If you love traveling, you'll want to have a travel budget. If you love music and concerts, you'll want to have a portion of your budget set aside for concerts and music festivals. What you prioritize in your budget will be different from other people.

Of course, travel and concerts fall into the "wants" portion of expenses, but I like to point out that working into your budget things that you enjoy doing is just as important as ensuring you include your necessary expenses and savings. Financial management is hard enough without feeling like you need to give up everything you love.

A budget does require some willpower and accountability. If you set money aside monthly for shopping and spend it all in the first week of the month, you can't dip into your savings, or your trust fund to keep shopping the rest of the month.

This is why budgeting is a key component of financial management, as it serves dual purposes. The first is to understand where your money is coming from and to know where it is going, as well as your necessary expenses. The second is to help teach financial accountability and restraint.

2. Saving

Saving is the process of setting aside money for future use rather than spending it immediately. This can include short-term savings for emergencies or unexpected expenses and long-term savings for goals such as retirement, education, or purchasing a home. Financially literate individuals understand the importance of saving regularly and the power of compound interest in growing their savings over time. They also explore different saving strategies, such as setting up automatic transfers to a savings account, utilizing employer-sponsored retirement plans, or investing in low-risk instruments like certificates of deposit or high-yield savings accounts.

Watching the money in your savings account grow over time through regular, automatic contributions and compound interest can be very gratifying.

Having unspent money in your account or trust fund isn't the same as having savings. Savings should be intentional. It should be a portion of money set aside for a specific purpose, even if that purpose is an emergency scenario that never manifests itself.

3. Investing

Investing involves putting money into assets with the expectation of generating returns over time. These assets can include stocks, bonds, mutual funds, real estate, or other financial instruments. Financially literate individuals understand the basics of investing, including risk and return, diversification, and the impact of inflation on investment returns. They also assess their risk tolerance and investment goals to develop a well-rounded investment portfolio that aligns with their objectives. Regularly monitoring investments and making adjustments as needed is also a key aspect of investing wisely.

I developed unhealthy spending habits when I received my first chunk of money from my trust fund. My trust fund installments meant a lot more money in my hands that could be spent unwisely if I wasn't careful. I didn't want to make the wrong decisions like I'd seen other people do, so I turned to investment opportunities. I used 95% of that first installment as the down payment on my house. It meant I didn't have direct access to those funds, but it also put them into an asset that could benefit me in multiple ways.

With that significant down payment, I had a large equity stake in the house, which would only grow based on the market I invested in.

It is worth mentioning that real estate investments depend on time and location. Not all real estate purchases are a good investment. If you're thinking of investing in real estate, just like with financial literacy in general, you'll want to familiarize yourself with real estate terminology and market trends and look at the best risk/reward situations.

I was fortunate enough to buy a good condo in a good buyer's market, which has benefited me ever since. The rental income I get from that unit helps pay a significant portion of my living expenses, and the value of the condo has already increased substantially, which I will receive if I ever decide to sell it. Right now, I'm holding onto it because I still get enough day-to-day value from the rental income, and there are a lot of ways to leverage a real estate asset without selling it.

If you're looking into investing, it's important to know the terminology for different fields. Stock market investments and real estate investments are going to be very different. The terminology, trends, and etiquette will vary. You don't need to become an investing master, but knowing your options and educating yourself on the best avenues available to you can go a long way to maintaining and growing your wealth.

4. Borrowing

Borrowing refers to obtaining funds from lenders with the agreement to repay the borrowed amount, typically with interest, over time. This can include borrowing money through loans, credit cards, mortgages, or lines of credit. Financially literate individuals understand the terms and conditions of borrowing, including interest rates, repayment schedules, and potential fees. They evaluate their borrowing needs carefully and avoid taking on excessive debt that could strain their finances. They also prioritize paying off high-interest debt and managing their credit responsibly to maintain a good credit score.

It's hard to imagine having to borrow money if you have a trust fund. It does happen. Some inheritors spend their money quickly. Then, to maintain appearances or a way of life, or even to keep up with expenses, they'll borrow money, max out credit cards and take out loans just to cover themselves.

Most of the time, they don't do it with the intention of getting deeper into debt. They think they'll be able to use that borrowed money to turn things around and grow their wealth again. Unfortunately, without the proper understanding of interest rates and repayment schedules, or the financial literacy to budget and leverage that money, they end up deeper in debt.

I don't want you to think that borrowing is all doom and gloom. It has huge benefits as long as you understand what you're getting into and what your responsibilities will be for paying the money back.

5. Managing Debt

Managing debt involves effectively handling any money owed to creditors. This includes making timely payments on debts, minimizing interest costs, and reducing debt balances over time. Financially literate individuals develop strategies for managing their debt, such as creating a debt repayment plan, prioritizing high-interest debt, and negotiating with creditors for better terms. They also avoid accumulating new debt unnecessarily and seek ways to improve their overall financial health, such as increasing income or cutting expenses to allocate more funds toward debt repayment.

Debt is a rather loaded word that is used in a lot of ways. If you have a car payment, a mortgage, student loans, or a monthly credit card balance, those are all debt. So, whether you have a small amount of debt, are in substantial debt, or are completely debt-free, it is still a part of financial literacy and management.

It is better to know how to manage debt before you have it so it doesn't get out of control.

By embracing these five key principles of financial literacy, you gain the ability to utilize money wisely, make well-informed financial choices, establish budgets, handle debt effectively, and strategize for your financial well-being in the long term. Take control of your finances and empower yourself with the knowledge to make the most of your inheritance.

FINANCIAL MANAGEMENT FOR INHERITORS

The five key components of financial literacy and wealth management apply universally to everyone. As I said, it could apply to a paycheck or a trust fund. However, as a trust funder, additional considerations must be considered when approaching financial literacy and wealth management. To simplify things, consider starting with the following three actions:

1. Wealth Assessment

For inheritors, assessing their finances involves a thorough examination of various aspects to ensure effective management and planning for the future. Firstly, reviewing assets is essential. This includes evaluating properties, investments, trusts, and any inheritances received. Understanding these assets' value and potential growth provides a clear picture of your overall financial portfolio.

Distinguishing between earned and unearned income streams is also crucial. Inheritors often receive income from investments or trust distributions, which differs from income earned through employment or business ventures. Recognizing your sources and these income streams' stability helps create a sustainable financial plan.

Another important step is analyzing spending habits and lifestyle costs. Inheritors should assess their expenses to identify areas where they can optimize spending and ensure that lifestyle costs align with their financial goals. This process enables them to maintain a balanced budget and allocate resources effectively.

Furthermore, clarifying goals for wealth is vital. Inheritors may have various objectives, such as wealth growth, philanthropic endeavors, or establishing a lasting legacy. Defining these goals helps develop a strategic financial plan tailored to their aspirations and values.

Knowing your purpose from the previous chapter can help in your wealth assessment. Since your financial goals may directly tie into your purpose, it can be a helpful component of figuring out where your money should be spent or allocated in alignment with that purpose.

In summary, you can assess finances by reviewing assets, understanding income streams, analyzing spending habits, and clarifying goals for wealth. This comprehensive approach facilitates informed decision-making and enables you to manage your finances effectively for present and future needs.

2. Creating a Budget

Creating a budget is crucial for inheritors to manage their finances wisely and achieve their financial goals. First and foremost, categorizing expenses into needs versus wants is essential. Needs are necessities like housing, food, and utilities, while wants are non-essential items like entertainment and luxury purchases. By distinguishing between the two, inheritors can prioritize spending on essential items and allocate funds more efficiently.

The next thing you'll need to do is establish a savings target percentage. Inheritors should determine how much of their monthly income they want to save or invest. This could be a fixed percentage or a specific amount that aligns with their financial goals and long-term plans. Setting aside savings regularly helps build a financial safety net and contributes to wealth accumulation over time.

Tracking expenditures is another crucial item you need to consider for informed decision-making. Inheritors should monitor their spending habits to identify areas where they can cut back or reallocate funds. By keeping a record of expenditures, they can better understand their financial priorities and adjust as needed to stay within their budget.

Finally, modeling different scenarios and tradeoffs allows inheritors to anticipate future financial needs and make strategic decisions. They can explore various scenarios, such as increasing savings or adjusting spending in different categories, to understand the potential impact on their overall financial situation. This helps them make informed choices about allocating resources effectively and achieving their financial objectives.

Setting realistic goals and timelines is another crucial aspect of managing money wisely. Inheritors should establish clear, achievable financial objectives aligning with their values and priorities. By setting realistic timelines for achieving these goals, inheritors can stay motivated and track their progress over time, adjusting their strategies as needed to stay on course.

3. Managing Wisely

Managing finances wisely as an inheritor involves several key strategies to ensure long-term financial security and fulfillment of personal goals. Firstly, investing in steady, responsible growth over time is crucial. Inheritors should build a diversified investment portfolio that balances risk and return to achieve sustainable long-term growth.

Working with advisors aligned with your values is an essential second step. Inheritors should seek out financial professionals who understand their priorities, goals, and ethical considerations. Collaborating with advisors who share their values ensures that investment strategies and decisions are in line with their overall vision for wealth management.

The third item to address is earning income through purpose-driven work that can provide a sense of fulfillment beyond financial gain. Inheritors may choose to engage in endeavors that align with their passions and values, generating income while positively impacting society or the environment.

Planning for impactful charitable giving allows inheritors to contribute to causes they care about and create a meaningful legacy. By setting aside funds for philanthropy and strategically allocating donations, they can make a difference in their communities and leave a lasting impact on the world.

Last but not least, passing on wealth judiciously to future generations involves careful estate planning and wealth transfer strategies. Inheritors should consider their heirs' needs and aspirations while ensuring the preservation and growth of family wealth for future generations.

In my situation, I knew that my trust fund wasn't enough to set me up for life, but I didn't know how I could maximize it as a resource. Part of that includes growing my wealth for a stable financial future and even thinking about what I'll leave behind to my heirs and future generations. It's never too early to start thinking about what you can leave behind.

GROW YOUR TRUST AND SET UP FUTURE GENERATIONS

Some good, universal practices can help you optimize your inheritance and set things in motion for the next generation.

Diversifying your portfolio and putting money away where it can't be easily accessed and freely spent is important for long-term financial stability. A diverse portfolio would include multiple types of investments, such as owning real estate, stock market investments, purchasing fine art, jewelry, etc. Inheritors should spread their investments across various asset classes to minimize risk and protect against market volatility.

If the housing market falls, you can still have assets in the stock market or other areas to compensate for that dip. However, having all your investment power in real estate is like having all your eggs in one basket. It's a much higher risk. Additionally, there are other places to set aside funds in less liquid assets or trust structures that can help safeguard wealth and ensure it remains intact for the intended purposes.

Building net worth through strategic financial management is a critical priority for inheritors seeking to optimize their wealth accumulation and financial security. Maximizing returns on investments is essential.

Inheritors should carefully evaluate investment opportunities and strategies to ensure they are maximizing their potential for growth and income.

This may involve diversifying investments across various asset classes, conducting thorough research, and actively monitoring market trends to identify opportunities for growth. Inheritors should spread their investments across various asset classes, industries, and geographic regions to reduce exposure to market fluctuations and potential losses. Diversification helps ensure a balance between risk and return, optimizing the potential for long-term investment growth while minimizing overall portfolio volatility.

My dad relied primarily on his trust with very little diversification of his assets or income. He did, however, buy a handful of properties throughout his life. I remember when the housing and stock market crashed in 2008, he went through periods of immeasurable stress that I know took a toll on his health. He died the next year, and while there were other factors that contributed to his death, that stress didn't help him. It might not have hit him so hard if he'd spread his investments out and had other assets to fall back on.

When inheriting money or assets, it is easy to become reliant on that wealth. That reliance is one factor behind never establishing an identity or purpose and succumbing to the psychological impacts of generational wealth.

Building financial independence is essential for inheritors as it encompasses several key aspects. It involves reducing reliance on inherited wealth by diversifying income sources and accumulating personal assets through various means such as employment, entrepreneurship, or investments. This provides greater financial stability and empowers individuals to make decisions aligned with their financial goals, values, and purpose.

Financial independence cultivates a sense of responsibility and self-sufficiency by encouraging inheritors to take ownership of their financial futures. This includes actively managing finances, setting goals, and making strategic decisions about saving, investing, and spending.

As a result, individuals develop important life skills and build resilience in the face of financial challenges. Financial independence enables individuals to pursue personal fulfillment and aspirations without being constrained by financial limitations. Whether it's pursuing passions, traveling, or giving back to communities, financial independence provides the freedom to pursue meaningful experiences and goals.

Lastly, building financial independence helps mitigate risks associated with potential loss or depletion of inherited assets. By diversifying assets, establishing emergency funds, and developing robust financial plans, inheritors can better withstand financial shocks and protect long-term financial security. Prioritizing financial independence ensures inheritors can create a solid foundation for long-term success, autonomy, and fulfillment in their lives.

Leveraging inherited assets to generate additional income streams is a strategic approach for inheritors to increase their net worth. My sister did this by investing in her husband's company, and I did the same when I used my trust money to buy a house. I leveraged one asset—my trust fund—to increase my net worth by adding to my portfolio a house that increases in value.

In addition to passive income generated from inherited assets, inheritors can explore opportunities to leverage their wealth through investments in income-producing assets such as real estate, dividend-paying stocks, or private equity. By strategically leveraging inherited assets, inheritors can enhance their financial resources and accelerate wealth accumulation.

Ignoring the importance of ongoing financial education is a common pitfall that inheritors must overcome. In today's rapidly changing financial landscape, staying informed and educated about financial matters is essential for making informed decisions and adapting to evolving market conditions.

Inheritors should prioritize ongoing financial education by reading books, attending seminars, and seeking advice from financial professionals. By continuously learning and staying informed, inheritors can enhance their financial literacy, make smarter financial choices, and avoid common pitfalls that could derail their financial success.

Nadia told me that when she decided to become an entrepreneur and start a business, she knew she had a safety net with her trust fund. As a result, she never felt pushed to do more with her business because she had a cushion from her bills always being paid. The business was more like something to do for fun. She didn't educate herself on how to make the business self-sustainable or profitable.

She would spend $15,000 on her yoga business in a year and only make $10,000 back. It was being run with a constant deficit. I always recommend consulting a professional financial advisor before making any decisions about your money. Even after you've done the research and educated yourself, having a second opinion from a professional is a great way to ensure you're making the best decisions to achieve your financial goals.

Inheritors face a lot of challenges when it comes to their wealth. I discussed the impacts of generational trauma and the psychology of inherited wealth earlier. Believe it or not, financial decision-making and management are particularly complicated for inheritors.

External influences and misconceptions about wealth can further complicate financial decision-making. Societal norms, cultural expectations, and media portrayals of wealth can foster unrealistic expectations and fuel a desire for extravagant spending. Misconceptions about the ease of managing wealth or the certainty of financial prosperity may lead to complacency and a lack of financial preparedness.

The risk of overspending and potentially depleting assets is a significant concern for inheritors. Despite inheriting substantial wealth, trust funders and inheritors are not immune to the consequences of poor financial habits. Lifestyle inflation, overspending, and a lack of financial discipline can erode wealth over time, leading to financial distress and diminished opportunities for financial recovery. While specific statistics about inheritors going broke may be challenging to obtain, my family's experiences and the experiences of those I work with make clear the importance of addressing these challenges through comprehensive financial education, prudent financial planning, and responsible stewardship of wealth.

If you're already blessed with wealth or an inheritance, I'd consider looking toward the future and what you can leave behind for future generations as part of your financial management. I say this because my father had all the means necessary to set up a substantial, growing financial portfolio, but he lacked the understanding of how to do it or how to include it in his financial management plan.

My dad bought and sold a handful of different homes and properties. Rather than hold onto them when he didn't need them anymore, he chose to sell each one and then buy a new one. He didn't need the money for a down payment or anything else—he simply didn't see the point in holding onto them long term. He didn't have the knowledge he needed to make real estate investing work for him.

In some situations, by the time he sold the property it was worth significantly more than when he bought it. Over the years, those properties have increased by over 1,000%. I tracked down one of the properties he purchased. He bought 17 acres for just under $700,000 in the early 80s.

In 2019, just a couple of acres that were separated from that same property sold for almost seven million dollars.

If my dad had held onto those properties in order to rent them out and had maintained his equity in them, he could have set up another handful of generations on his own. Like many people, he didn't have the knowledge or understanding to do that. As one of my mentors says, "Only buy, never sell." My dad's situation was a good example of that.

There are many ways to build generational wealth:

1. Invest in the stock market: The stock market is a way to build wealth passively. It can also protect your money from inflation. A long-term stock market investment plan can accumulate vast amounts of wealth over several years, even decades, to set your children up with a growing, sustainable asset.

2. Invest in real estate: Real estate is a great tool for building wealth, as exemplified by what I'm doing with my house and what my father could have done with his properties. Real estate generally appreciates over time, even with market crashes like the one that occurred in 2008. Depending on what kind of real estate you invest in, it can also provide income streams and cash flow. Nadia thinks there are some opportunities she didn't take because of her inheritance and her lack of understanding when it came to financial management. Ten years ago, she considered buying a house in Portugal when she had the money. She thinks of a lot of different opportunities she could have invested in when the funds were there. While she did invest in her education and business, she didn't take advantage of opportunities to make any long-term investments. She took for granted that the money would be there. Now, she thinks she has lost the opportunity to make some good long-term investments. When she turned 29, the money was gone. She had no clue what to do

anymore and knew she wasn't going to teach yoga or be able to scale her business. She said she totally shut that door. Then she turned 30, and suddenly she knew what she wanted. She says that her views on money have changed over the years. She's looking more at long-term investments and not putting things off. She told herself she'd buy a house by the time she was 33, and she closed on a condo a few months before she turned 34. Her next goal is to buy land. Spending her trust money has inspired and motivated her to make smarter choices, diversify her portfolio, and make these investments to build her wealth again.

3. Create a business to pass down: About 30% of family-owned businesses make it to the second generation.[70] Not all wealth or assets are passed down in the form of bank accounts or trust funds. A business also has a net worth and can be an avenue for passing down wealth to your children. Whether they choose to take over the business themselves, hire someone to manage it for them in order to create a passive stream of income, or sell it in order to pursue their own purpose, a business can provide different forms of generational wealth.

Once you have established wealth to pass down, you'll also want to think about how to pass it down in the event of death or incapacitation. You want to know beforehand that your assets will be divided according to your wishes.

The most common ways to pass down wealth include:

*   Write a will
*   Set up a trust
*   Name account beneficiaries

Whatever route you choose for setting up the transfer of wealth, I advise speaking to a professional estate planner or attorney first. They can help you settle things based on your wishes, talk you through the best options that work for you and your assets, and prevent the headaches of probate and high taxation on inheritance assets that aren't in a trust.

In the same way that financial literacy and management require self-education, knowledge, and planning, setting up transferable wealth requires the same things. The bottom line is that when you educate yourself on financial literacy and maximize your assets for yourself and your children, you gain a level of empowerment and control of your own financial destiny.

With hindsight, we can almost all look back and think about how we would have done things differently or made better choices. One of the purposes of this book is to help people with what they are experiencing now so that they don't have to rely on hindsight and witnessing mistakes to do better going forward.

For more customized tools and resources on Financial Literacy and Financial Management, visit trustyourtrustfund.com.

CHAPTER 7
BUILDING A LIFE BEYOND MONEY

One of the healthiest things inheritors can do is build a life beyond money. This relates to establishing your own identity and finding your purpose. Once you have that independence and separation from your wealth, life itself is more fulfilling, and you aren't defined by your inheritance or the values and expectations of your family.

When you discover more meaningful ways of living through intentional action and aligning with your purpose, you leap forward with a more fulfilling life.

Two defining factors made me evaluate my life and figure out what I needed to do for myself beyond my money. The first factor was that I knew I wasn't ready to manage the large sum of money that came to me from my first large trust fund installment. I had to explore alternatives, like real estate. This pushed me to look beyond money as a consumable resource and see what else was out there for me.

The second factor was my pursuit of starting a coaching business. I knew it was what I wanted, and it aligned with my values, but because I didn't need the money I felt no urgency to follow that path. So, I made the decision to cut myself off from my trust fund, quite literally looking at how to build a life beyond my money. I had been receiving a monthly distribution to pay my bills. I emailed my trustees and advisors to let them know I didn't need monthly distributions for the foreseeable future.

Because of the way the trust is set up, I couldn't give the money away or do anything that my trustees wouldn't approve, but I did have the ability to cut off monthly distributions to my personal checking. I was already in a position to understand the value of a dollar because of my upbringing, but cutting myself off was precisely the kick in the butt I needed to get myself on track with a fulfilling, profitable career.

As it turned out, as soon as I limited my access to my trust, I landed a coaching job that paid—to the cent—the same amount that I'd been using from my trust monthly to cover my cost of living.

It wasn't an easy decision, but I'm glad I made it because it gave me the chance to explore my values, establish my identity, and see what life could be without defining myself by my trust.

THE WHEEL OF LIFE

Money is only one area of life that impacts our mental health and prosperity. In fact, it is just one of eight parts of the wheel of life. The wheel of life, which was created by Paul J. Meyer, is a tool coaches use to map the major components of our human experience. The wheel includes health/well-being, significant other and romance, friends and family, fun and leisure, personal growth and learning, home environment, spirituality, and, yes, money. When you analyze happiness and fulfillment in life, it is important to measure your satisfaction with each of these areas because they contribute to our daily lives and overall well-being.

Surprisingly, many people with trust funds or who've inherited assets—though they might be well off when it comes to money—don't always rate the money section of the wheel as providing a high level of satisfaction. This furthers the argument that money isn't the key to happiness or fulfillment, and it shows that relationships with money are more complicated than simply having access to it.

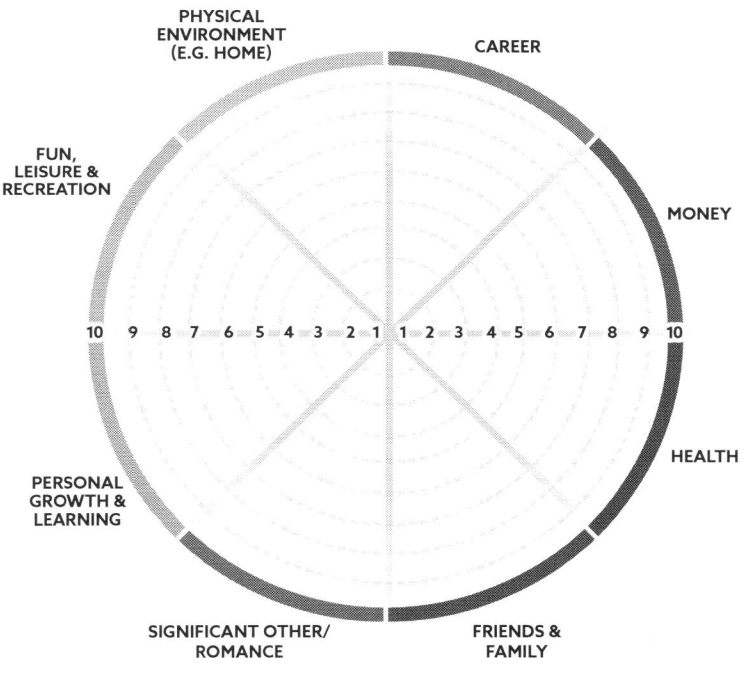

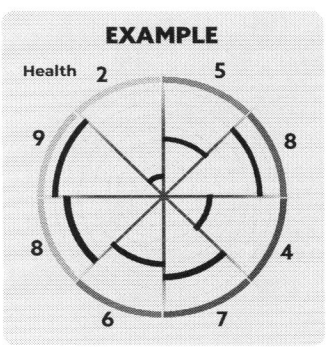

It is my recommendation that you look at those eight segments on the wheel of life and rate your satisfaction level with each one from 1 to 10. Any area that rates a 6 or lower is an area of your life that could and should be improved in order for you to strive for a happy and fulfilling life.

When I say "building a life beyond money," I think of my sisters and the paths they've taken.

One of my sisters used her trust fund to put herself through medical school. It was a smart decision, but she's gone through a lot of personal development and has found a balance between what she wants and where the money led her. Now, she's a practicing naturopathic doctor, which aligns a lot more with her personal values and what she wants out of life. In essence, her money is what enabled her to have a career as a doctor. The money had always defined her and the path she took in life. Years later, she was able to look at choosing a different path beyond the money, and it has led her to a far more fulfilling career.

My other sister, who invested in her husband's company, chose to focus on her family rather than her finances. She's primarily a stay-at-home mom, and she loves it. With her trust fund, she could have gone to school, established herself in a lucrative career, or followed the path of the partying rich and famous. With the success her husband has created, she could have hired a full-time nanny, like our grandparents did for my father. But her values and dreams didn't lie with her career or money.

Both of my sisters are great examples of not settling for what was expected of them because of their circumstances. They stepped away from societal and familial stigmas to build a life beyond their money.

Inheritance isn't just money, though. I spoke to a gentleman whose inheritance came to him in the form of business assets. He had a very different upbringing with his inheritance.

David, another inheritor I spoke to, has wealth and experience from inheriting a fortune from a family business, which also comes with responsibility. While he's made a fortune for himself, there have been some ups and downs and struggles along the way, especially since he learned what wealth could do by seeing the mistakes his friends and family made.

David is a fifth-generation inheritor. From a young age, he knew he'd be part of a big family business. When he was only 13, he settled estates for his grandfather and grandmother. He even developed his dad's estate plan. He learned a lot from watching his parents and grandparents, but he also had an eclectic educational background that led him to personal success.

His parents also traveled with him all over the world at an early age. Those trips taught him a lot about culture, history, and art. He learned lessons about family successes and mistakes that would later help guide him.

When David was seven or eight years old, he was informed of his family's position and his inheritance. It was hard to avoid since he grew up in the small town where his family's principal offices and factories were. He'd go down to the offices and spend time with his mom and dad there. His mother was his father's secretary, so business was a prominent part of his family dynamic whether he was at the office or at home.

His grandmother lived with him and his parents until she passed away, and she always had a strong connection to the business. He said if he'd woken up one random morning to learn that his grandfather was a Pillsbury, or someone knocked on the door and handed him an inheritance that he never knew he was part of, it would have been a very different experience. Instead, for him the family business and wealth were intimate.

David felt no real separation between himself, his family, and the family business in his youth. Establishing an identity and a life outside of them all can be hard.

As inheritors, we are blessed to have the resources for opportunity. With that comes the ability to literally create the life we want for ourselves. It is up to us to determine what that life looks like.

Building a fulfilling life for trust funders and inheritors beyond financial wealth involves planning, self-discovery, and a commitment to personal growth. Think about yourself as an individual, separate from any family expectations or values you've been raised with.

Here are some steps and considerations:

- Clarify your values: Understand what truly matters to you beyond material wealth. Reflect on your passions, interests, and principles. Doing so will serve as a foundation for building a meaningful life.
- Set personal goals: Identify goals that align with your values and interests. These goals could be related to personal development, career aspirations, philanthropy, or creative pursuits.
- Seek meaningful work: Instead of relying solely on your inheritance, explore opportunities for meaningful work or entrepreneurship. Engaging in work that you find fulfilling can provide a sense of purpose and achievement.
- Education and skill development: Invest in education and skill development to enhance your capabilities and pursue your interests. This could involve formal education, vocational training, or self-directed learning. Focus on courses or training programs that align with your hobbies and interests.
- Embrace philanthropy: Consider how you can use your resources to positively impact causes that are important to you. Engaging in philanthropy can bring a sense of fulfillment and contribute to positive change in the world.
- Cultivate relationships: Build meaningful connections with family, friends, mentors, and communities. Relationships provide

support, guidance, and opportunities for personal growth.

- Practice financial literacy: While financial wealth may not be your primary focus, it's essential to have a basic understanding of personal finance. This includes budgeting, investing, and managing assets responsibly.
- Embrace lifelong learning: Stay curious and open to new experiences. Continuously seek opportunities for learning and personal growth, whether through travel, hobbies, or exploration of different cultures and perspectives.
- Maintain Balance: Strive for balance in all aspects of your life, including work, relationships, leisure, and personal development. Avoid becoming consumed by financial concerns or external expectations.
- Seek professional guidance: Consider working with financial advisors, career coaches, or therapists who specialize in working with inheritors. They can provide tailored guidance and support as you navigate your unique circumstances.

Remember that building a fulfilling life is a journey, and it's okay to reassess your priorities and goals along the way. By cultivating self-awareness, pursuing your passions, and making intentional choices, you can create a life that is rich in meaning and fulfillment beyond financial wealth.

With the variety of available inheritance setups, sometimes the system itself almost unintentionally promotes unhealthy relationships between family members and money. David told me about a friend who has cousins who depend on dividends from a parent company to be the trust fund. He said it seems unhealthy to be relying on "Cousin Ethel" to turn a profit at the family company because you're benefiting from her. And it puts both "Ethel" and the cousins in an unhealthy relationship with each other and the money.

David says he's fortunate never to have faced that. His grandfather set it up that way. His father didn't face it, he didn't, and now his kids won't either.

But more estates than not are set up the other way around. You're going to continue to be a minority shareholder. Your uncle or cousin, or whoever, is going to work their ass off, and you're inevitably going to whine about wanting larger dividends. So, how do you separate yourself from that?

The coaching path I started out on has evolved and morphed and now takes me in a new direction. I don't think that what I was doing before wasn't part of my purpose. As my purpose changes, so does the path I need to follow for fulfillment. This reassessment might happen every couple of years, or it could happen less frequently.

When you do reassess, look at the entire wheel of life again. Don't limit your assessment to your career or any one segment of the wheel.

A RICH LIFE

In a culture where instant gratification reigns supreme, it's crucial to acknowledge a fundamental truth—true wealth and success aren't achieved in a flash. Consider the timeless tale of the tortoise and the hare—the slow and steady pace often leads to victory. It's about forgoing that daily cup of coffee, dedicating an extra hour to learning, and making consistent, incremental choices that accumulate over time. Rather than banking on luck or quick fixes, persistence and diligence pave the path to enduring prosperity.

Jessie O'Neill stated, "Those who have attained great wealth, inherited money or spend their lives chasing it, often lose the very joy that makes life truly 'rich'—loving, lasting relationships with our families and friends, spirituality, and the balance and self-fulfillment that comes with the knowledge that it is truly better to give than to receive."[71]

Growing up, I held onto the notion that a "rich life" equated to owning grand mansions and driving flashy luxury cars. However, with age and experience, my perspective shifted. I came to understand that genuine wealth transcends material possessions—it resides in the richness of experiences, meaningful relationships, and continual personal development. It's about awakening each day with a sense of purpose, indulging in life without the weight of guilt, and staying true to one's core values. While money may provide comfort, the true essence of a rich life lies in the intentional cultivation of one's journey.

It might not provide the instant dopamine rush that buying an expensive new pair of shoes or going on a luxury vacation gives you, but in the long term, fulfillment, abundance, and prosperity don't come from material wealth, possessions, or the "rich life" that is portrayed in the media.

Experiences hold a distinct advantage over spending money, as they offer lasting value and enrichment to our lives. Unlike material possessions that depreciate over time, experiences often appreciate in value as cherished memories. They foster personal growth, broaden perspectives, and strengthen relationships in ways that material goods cannot. Investing in experiences allows us to create meaningful connections, savor the present moment, and cultivate a more fulfilling life. In the end, the experiences that we accumulate are the things that genuinely enrich our journey and define our sense of fulfillment.

In David's family's history, they had made and lost three great fortunes. It was the nature of business—fortunes rise and fall. He said that one of those falls was on his watch.

When I asked David about the rise and fall of his family fortune, he told me the stories of what went wrong. In 1912, his great-uncle bought Brazilian bonds and lost the fortune his great-grandfather made. Then, his father got caught in the depression and lost the fortune his grandfather made. David himself got stuck in the Asian economic bubble and lost the fortune that his father made. He says they've all been fortunate to make the money back, which doesn't always happen.

David says that his family prevailed based on fundamental principles. He thinks it comes from generating wealth through business rather than the wealth inventoried five generations prior. If you don't work in the business, you don't benefit from the business.

Part of what it comes down to also, David said, is the mindset. He says that his family never thinks of themselves as "down." They think of it as preparing for the next act. Mindset is a very powerful asset when thinking about finances.

He also explained how he felt about the word *pity* and why it's such a harsh word. He lamented for his friends who are not in the trenches with their businesses and who will miss the thrill of victory, the agony of defeat, and the thrill of resurrection. David lives that. He says he doesn't wish for his son or daughter to fail, but when he was coaching MBA students at Stanford University, he recalls saying, "Fail early, fail forward, and fail fearlessly."

Despite being related to the family business, these core values and personal goals held by David and his predecessors helped shape the future of their company and family. His philosophy on being in the trenches, failing forward, and rising up are inspiring traits that have given David a full, meaningful life in areas outside his business—like in the relationships with the basketball players he coached.

Relationships, whether with family, friends, or romantic partners, are another aspect of wealth and prosperity that provides an advantage over expenses, material items, and financial wealth. We are social creatures, and having a support system of like-minded people—someone to share our life experiences with, and loved ones we can turn to, count on, and relate to—is powerful when it comes to fulfillment.

Wealth and finances can often get in the way of solid and meaningful connections and relationships. My dad struggled to have a solid circle of friends he trusted and could count on because he was concerned about people taking advantage of his kindness and wealth.

I've witnessed other situations where money can cause friction in romantic relationships. Whether it is an abundance of money or a lack of money, finances can influence the dynamics of how people connect.

Even within my own family, there have been strains due to money. After my uncle passed away and left his assets to me and my siblings, other relatives—an aunt, and an uncle—felt like they were left out of his will. They thought they were entitled to some of his assets despite his wishes. As a result, it has created strain between those family members and all of us who were named in the will.

When the focus is on financial gain or financial and material wealth, experiences, relationships, and personal development get out of balance. All the areas on the wheel are represented in equal proportions. No single area is more important than the other. You can think about it in terms of an actual wheel with spokes. If one spoke is longer than the others, or if they are all different lengths, the wheel won't turn properly or bear weight.

In terms of life, if your wheel of life isn't balanced, the same thing can happen. That's why it's important to establish satisfaction in each of those areas. I'd like to note that your level of satisfaction in one area might differ from someone else's. Some people want to put more focus on their family or their career. They can still be fulfilled in other areas without putting as much focus on them. Your wheel is personal to you and your goals, interests, and purpose.

That said, it still requires balance for holistic prosperity and a rich life.

CULTIVATING TRUE WEALTH

In a society that frequently equates success with financial prosperity, it's crucial to recognize that true wealth extends far beyond mere monetary abundance. Genuine wealth transcends the confines of a bank balance. While some may accumulate substantial riches, they often discover their lives are deficient in other vital facets like meaningful relationships, well-being, and the freedom to pursue their passions.

Part of this can come from familial influences, so finding your purpose and identity is a major step in cultivating a rich life beyond money.

It's common to witness individuals attaining financial triumph while grappling with challenges in other spheres of their lives. While pursuing monetary goals is significant, it shouldn't overshadow our health, relationships, or overall welfare.

When David started working at the company in 1980, he was also the president of the state historical society. He was an investor in a wine importation business and chairman of the Young Presidents' Organization chapter. He was also the chair of the board of trustees for Evergreen State College. All of that was going on while he was heading toward going broke. He says he was using those activities to compensate for a desire for creativity in his ecosystem—creativity that he wasn't getting by working at the family business. He had a very aware approach to creating a rich, full life for himself.

The way he sees it, money or inheritance shouldn't be an obstacle to pursuing what you want. He has a friend who grew up with a trust fund and is a gifted carpenter. He charges about $100,000 for cabinetry and has a year-long waiting list. A job like carpentry is often seen as menial or working class, but someone with a real gift for it and a head for business has turned his passion into something far more lucrative.

David pointed out that for some people, like Brittney's mom, a trust fund is an excuse to do nothing. But if you look at it the other way around, a trust fund affords you the ability to do anything you want. He thinks it is the responsibility of everyone who has wealth or substantial inheritance to do something.

Genuine wealth encompasses a holistic approach to encompass fulfillment in various aspects of life—it entails a multifaceted and enriching existence. This includes:

- Health: Vital for a truly prosperous life, good health forms the cornerstone of well-being. No amount of wealth can substitute for physical and mental wellness. Prioritizing your health is integral to genuine prosperity.
- Relationships: The value of meaningful connections with family, friends, and loved ones is immeasurable. Cultivating and cherishing these bonds adds richness and depth to life's experiences.
- Time: True wealth affords you the freedom to dictate your schedule rather than being enslaved by it. Achieving a harmonious balance between work and personal life and having the liberty to pursue your passions is essential for authentic prosperity.
- Purpose: Discovering and pursuing your life's purpose and contributing positively to your community or society is a fundamental aspect of true wealth. It transcends mere accumulation of riches, providing a sense of fulfillment and meaning beyond oneself.
- Balance is essential: Pursue equilibrium across various aspects of life, recognizing that success encompasses more than just financial achievements.

For his own health and pursuit of purpose, David was the first person in his family to work for someone else in a century.

Separating himself from his family business and venturing out on his own helped David establish his own confidence and drive to follow his own passions outside of his family business and legacy but it also gave him the skills and tools to serve his family legacy better.

Take a look at your own wheel of life and rate your levels of satisfaction in each area. Then, reflect back on the steps toward cultivating true wealth so you, too, can start building a rich, fulfilling life beyond money. When you have a more balanced, well-rounded life driven by purpose, experiences, relationships, and personal development, you might notice your relationship with money changes, too. You can develop a healthier, more positive relationship with money outside of guilt, shame, and the other complex emotions around inheritance.

For more customized tools and resources on
Building a Life Beyond Money, visit trustyourtrustfund.com.

CONCLUSION

Dear Reader,

When you receive an inheritance, it can be both a blessing and a curse. I experienced both sides of the equation with my own inheritance and through my family's experiences. On this journey, I realized that there is a lack of information and discussion around the topics that many inheritors hide or struggle with throughout their lives.

I wrote this book to shine a light on the underside of inheritance and how it can lead to complicated emotions like guilt and shame around inheriting money. In my experience, these emotions aren't openly discussed and are easily dismissed by society because there is the assumption that money can solve every problem.

We've explored how generational wealth can result in unhealed generational trauma that's passed down through the years and can cause problems for inheritors in current or future generations. Many times, those traumas are ingrained, and it is hard to unravel them because of their long-standing past.

For inheritors of generational wealth, it often comes with extreme expectations, feelings of inadequacy, and many other complicated emotions tied to family. Wealthy families can have their own culture, and sometimes that wealth can strain families, test their bonds, and cause a lot of entitlement and legal battles. We also discussed the common circumstance of family expectations when inheriting money or a business. These expectations can completely deter someone from following their true desires and goals in life.

For all inheritors, there can be concerns with money management. Money goes so quickly, and some people don't realize it until they control a large sum. Others worry about being taken advantage of, often leading to trust issues.

My personal journey opened my eyes to a lot of the hidden truths about inheritance with hard lessons I had to learn on my own. My hope is that by bringing these topics into the open and discussing them, stigmas around inherited wealth can be dispelled. I hope inheritors realize they don't have to struggle alone or in silence because there are a lot of us out there going through similar ups and downs.

I've spoken to several other people who were willing to share their stories about their own inheritance experiences, and who have faced similar challenges and emotional struggles. It's hard to reflect on those emotions and traumas to find the upside, but I don't want you to feel discouraged. It's never too late to turn things around or make a change for yourself. It's never too late to turn your inheritance into a blessing, whether it is through finding new opportunities, learning to manage your finances, or learning from your mistakes to make better choices.

I look at my mother's experience. She received a divorce settlement with my father and quickly blew through it. She went from riches to rags, but she learned from the experience and she drove forward. Now, she's more successful than ever and she did it all on her own.

So, whether you have a current inheritance, will be coming into one, or somehow lost one, it's never too late or too early to start making plans. In my experience, and in the experiences of those closest to me, when you take charge of your wealth and do something incredible with it, even if you have to build it back up from nothing, it leads to a far more fulfilling life than if you don't do anything with it at all.

Throughout this book, you were asked many self-reflection questions and given some new perspectives on how to handle and view your inheritance. You're ready to take the next steps in managing your wealth and creating a fulfilling future.

When you're ready to take the next steps in your journey, find me at trustyourtrustfund.com. You can contact me directly and take advantage of the free companion information I have available.

Thank you for reading my book. I'm looking forward to connecting.

Chase

ACKNOWLEDGMENTS

I would like to thank my family. Mom, without you, I wouldn't be half the human I am today. You were always there for me and showed me more love and support than I could ask for. You are the best mother and friend anyone could ask for. You've given me the strength and courage to heal, grow, and follow my dreams.

My siblings, without your friendships this book would not be possible. You guys showed so much support and love through this process of sharing our story. You were open and receptive to anything I brought to the table. I am forever grateful for the relationships we have together.

Dad, although you haven't physically been here for a while, I still learn lessons from you daily. You were the brightest light and the best father, brother, son, and friend. To have known you was to love you. Thank you for the sacrifices you made and the strength you've passed on to your children.

Me and my dad on the lake.

Dad and his '72 Super Sport Chevelle. We still have this car today!

The family in Chicago in 2001.

Me and my siblings. Thankful to have a best friend in each of them!

My sister and I, running around since day one.

My sisters and I pictured with Uncle Will in Florida.

My parents on their wedding day.

Me and my mom at my grandma's in Chicago. I
couldn't ask for a more loving, supportive mom.

My dad, Will, and their parents on the family island.

My dad, brother, and I tubing in Florida. A very memorable day

BIBLIOGRAPHY

Assylzhan, Izbassar, Muragul Muratbekova, Daniyar Amangeldi, Nazzere Oryngozha, Anna Ogorodova, and Pakizar Shamoi. "Intelligent System for Assessing University Student Personality Development and Career Readiness." *Procedia Computer Science* 231 (2024): 779–785. https://doi.org/10.48550/arXiv.2308.15620.

Brower, Tracy. "Purpose May Be the Key to Happiness: 3 Reasons Why." *Forbes*, March 19, 2023. https://www.forbes.com/sites/tracybrower/2023/03/19/purpose-may-be-the-key-to-happiness-3-reasons-why/.

Bundick, Matthew J., Kathleen Remington, Emily Morton, and Anne Colby. "The Contours of Purpose Beyond the Self in Midlife and Later Life." *Applied Developmental Science* 25, no. 1 (2019): 62–82. https://doi.org/10.1080/10888691.2018.1531718.

Chapple, Reshawna. "What Is Generational Trauma? Signs, Causes, & How to Heal." Talkspace, February 2, 2023. https://www.talkspace.com/blog/generational-trauma/.

Chen, James. "Sudden Wealth Syndrome (SWS): Definition, Causes, and Treatment." Investopedia, last modified September 1, 2024. https://www.investopedia.com/terms/s/suddenwealthsyndrome.asp.

Cobb, Lacey. "Sudden Wealth Syndrome & How to Avoid It." *The Currency*, Empower, June 10, 2021. https://www.empower.com/the-currency/life/sudden-wealth-syndrome-tips.

Cohen, Randy, Chirag Bavishi, and Alan Rozanski. "Purpose in Life and Its Relationship to All-Cause Mortality and Cardiovascular Events." *Psychosomatic Medicine* 78, no. 2 (2016): 149–158. https://doi.org/10.1097/PSY.0000000000000274.

Cole, Peter. "The Psychological Dynamics of Inherited Wealth." Street Directory, accessed September 4, 2024. https://www.streetdirectory.com/travel_guide/143282/how_to_grow_wealth/the_psychological_dynamics_of_inherited_wealth.html.

Csikszentmihalyi, Mihaly. "If We Are So Rich, Why Aren't We Happy?" *American Psychologist* 54, no. 10 (1999): 821–827. https://doi.org/10.1037/0003-066X.54.10.821.

Curtis, Tiffany. "How Generational Trauma Affects Your Finances and How to Heal." NerdWallet, November 2, 2022. https://www.nerdwallet.com/article/finance/generational-trauma.

Donnelly, Grant E., Tianyi Zheng, Emily Haisley, and Michael I. Norton. "The Amount and Source of Millionaires' Wealth (Moderately) Predict Their Happiness." *Personality & Social Psychology Bulletin* 44, no. 5 (2018): 684–699. https://doi.org/10.1177/0146167217744766.

Edmonds, Charlotte. "Here's How Much Money the Average NFL Player Makes in 2022." NBC Sports Philadelphia, July 29, 2022. https://www.nbcsportsphiladelphia.com/nfl/philadelphia-eagles/heres-how-much-money-the-average-nfl-player-makes-in-2022/250699/.

"Epigenetics." *Psychology Today*, accessed September 4, 2024. https://www.psychologytoday.com/us/basics/epigenetics.

Field, Jena. "The Science Behind Guilt and Shame." *The Monkey Therapist*, accessed September 4, 2024. https://themonkeytherapist.com/science-behind-guilt-shame/.

Frank, Sarah. "As Wealthy People, We Damn Well Better Be Funding Resource Generation Ourselves!" Resource Generation, November 27, 2017. https://resourcegeneration.org/as-wealthy-people-we-damn-well-better-be-funding-rg-ourselves/.

Gardner, Jonathan, and Andrew J. Oswald. "Money and Mental Wellbeing: A Longitudinal Study of Medium-sized Lottery Wins." *Journal of Health Economics* 26, no. 1 (2007): 49–60. https://doi.org/10.1016/j.jhealeco.2006.08.004.

Glicksman, Eve. "Your Brain on Guilt and Shame." BrainFacts.org, September 12, 2019. https://www.brainfacts.org/thinking-sensing-and-behaving/emotions-stress-and-anxiety/2019/your-brain-on-guilt-and-shame-091219.

Hegen, Derek. "How to Think About Wealth and Guilt." *Meaningful Money*, October 1, 2020. https://www.meaningfulmoney.life/post/wealth-guilt.

Hill, Patrick L., and Nicholas A. Turiano. "Purpose in Life as a Predictor of Mortality Across Adulthood." *Psychological Science* 25, no. 7 (2014): 1482–1486. https://doi.org/10.1177/0956797614531799.

Hill, Patrick L., Anthony L. Burrow, Jay W. Brandenberger, Daniel K. Lapsley, and Jessica Collado Quaranto. "Collegiate Purpose Orientations and Well-Being in Early and Middle Adulthood." *Journal of Applied Developmental Psychology* 31, no. 2 (2010): 173–179. https:// doi.org/10.1016/j.appdev.2009.12.001.

"Infographic: The Family Business—Successes and Obstacles," *Score*, June 13, 2024, https://www.score.org/resource/infographic/infographic -family-business—successes-and-obstacles.

"Inheriting a Fortune: Overcoming the Challenges of Sudden Wealth Syndrome." *FasterCapital*, last modified June 2, 2024. https:// fastercapital.com/content/Inheriting-a-Fortune--Overcoming-the-Challenges-of-Sudden-Wealth-Syndrome.html.

Kahneman, Daniel, and Angus Deaton. "High Income Improves Evaluation of Life But Not Emotional Well-Being." *Proceedings of the National Academy of Sciences of the United States of America* 107, no. 38 (2010): 16489–16493. https://doi.org/10.1073/pnas.1011492107.

Kim, Eric S., Koichiro Shiba, Julia K. Boehm, and Laura D. Kubzansky. "Sense of Purpose in Life and Five Health Behaviors in Older Adults." *Preventive Medicine* 139, no. 106172 (2020). https://doi.org/10.1016/j.ypmed.2020.106172.

Kirkland, Richard I., Jr. "Should You Leave It All to the Children?" *Fortune*, September 29, 1986. https://money.cnn.com/magazines/fortune/for-tune_archive/1986/09/29/68098/index.htm.

Miller, David. "The Common Misconceptions About a Wealthy Upbringing." *Psychology Today*, July 11, 2018. https://www.psychologytoday.com/us/blog/the-human-side-finance/201807/the-common-misconceptions-about-wealthy-upbringing.

"'My Trust Fund Made Me Miserable': Lucky Relatives Set to Inherit Millions Reveal How Their Wealth Makes Them Feel 'Guilty and Isolated.'" *Daily Mail*, last modified August 18, 2018. https://www.dailymail.co.uk/news/article-6071429/The-dark-guilty-lonely-having-million-dollar-trust-fund.html.

Nimmo, Karen. "Beyond Money: These Are the Six Things People Crave Most." *On the Couch*, Medium, August 22, 2022. https://medium.com/on-the-couch/beyond-money-these-are-the-six-things-people-crave-most-9664cd09c5be.

Ratner, Kaylin, Qingyi Li, Gaoxia Zhu, Melody Estevez, and Anthony L. Burrow. "Daily Adolescent Purposefulness, Daily Subjective Well-Being, and Individual Differences in Autistic Traits." *Journal of Happiness Studies* 24, no. 3 (2023): 967–989. https://doi.org/10.1007/s10902-023-00625-7.

Reynolds, Judy. "Unleashing the Power of Purpose: Leading a Life of Passion and Success." *Opening Gates*, July 14, 2023. https://opening-gates.com/unleashing-the-power-of-purpose-leading-a-life-of-passion-and-success/.

Ryder, Gina. "What Is Genetic Trauma?" PsychCentral, February 18, 2022. https://psychcentral.com/health/genetic-trauma.

Sands, Leo. "For Mega-Rich Heirs, the Anxieties That Drive 'Succession' Are All Too Real." *Washington Post*, last modified May 31, 2023. https://www.washingtonpost.com/wellness/2023/05/30/succession-wealth-family-life-psychologists/.

Schorsch, Irvin G., III. "Too Much Too Soon: How to Avoid Sudden Wealth Syndrome." *HuffPost*, last modified September 6, 2012. https://www.huffpost.com/entry/sudden-wealth-syndrome_b_1652701.

Serena. "The Power of Purpose: A Guided Journey to a Fulfilling Life." *Horizon Hub*, Medium, February 4, 2024. https://medium.com/horizon-hub/the-power-of-purpose-a-guided-journey-to-a-fulfilling-life-9c5c6d711be7.

Shan, Lee Ying. "'Wealth Can Be Pretty Isolating': Problems That Rich People Face, According to Therapists." CNBC, May 13, 2024. https://www.cnbc.com/2024/05/14/problems-that-rich-people-face-according-to-therapists-.html.

Sherman, Jeremy E. "How the Rich Cope with Shame About Their Unfair Advantage." *Psychology Today*, September 17, 2019. https://www.psychologytoday.com/us/blog/ambigamy/201909/how-the-rich-cope-shame-about-their-unfair-advantage.

Shiba, Koichiro, Laura D. Kubzansky, David R. Williams, Tyler J. VanderWeele, and Eric S. Kim. "Purpose in Life and 8-Year Mortality by Gender and Race/Ethnicity Among Older Adults in the U.S." *Preventive Medicine* 164, no. 107310 (2022). https://doi.org/10.1016/j.ypmed.2022.107310.

Simon-Thomas, Emiliana R. "How Strong Is Your Sense of Purpose in Life?" *Greater Good Magazine*, April 11, 2022. https://greatergood.berkeley.edu/article/item/how_strong_is_your_sense_of_purpose_in_life.

Sparks, Hannah. "My Trust Fund Made Me Miserable." *New York Post*, last modified August 20, 2018. https://nypost.com/2018/08/15/my-trust-fund-made-me-miserable/.

"Sudden Wealth Syndrome." Money Meaning & Choices Institute, accessed September 4, 2024, https://www.mmcinstitute.com/about-2/sudden-wealth-syndrome/.

Torre, Pablo S. "How (and Why) Athletes Go Broke." *Sports Illustrated*, March 23, 2009. https://vault.si.com/vault/2009/03/23/how-and-why-athletes-go-broke.

Vanderbilt, Arthur T., II. *Fortune's Children: The Fall of the House of Vanderbilt*. William Morrow, 2001.

Vega, Nicolas. "Anderson Cooper Won't Leave His Fortune to His Son: Why 'I Don't Believe in Passing on Huge Amounts of Money.'" *Make It*, CNBC, September 27, 2021. https://www.cnbc.com/2021/09/27/why-anderson-cooper-wont-leave-an-inheritance-for-his-son.html.

Walsh, Judy Lin, and Stephen Salley. "The Inheritance Effect." Banyan Global, accessed September 4, 2024. https://banyan.global/ideas/the-inheritance-effect/.

Watkin, Hannah. "Everything Anderson Cooper Has Said About His Son's $200 Million Inheritance." *Hello!*, July 24, 2023. https://www.hellomagazine.com/healthandbeauty/mother-and-baby/498400/anderson-cooper-sons-inheritance-everything-hes-said/.

"Wealth Guilt: What to Do When Your Child Is Ashamed of Your Family's Wealth." City National Bank, accessed September 4, 2024. https://www.cnb.com/private-banking/insights/wealth-guilt.html.

Wealth, Anne-Lyse. "Generational Wealth: What It Is & How to Build It." *The Currency*, Empower, January 31, 2023. https://www.empower.com/the-currency/money/how-to-build-generational-wealth.

Zimmerman, Rachel. "How Does Trauma Spill from One Generation to the Next?" *Washington Post*, June 12, 2023. https://www.washingtonpost.com/wellness/2023/06/12/generational-trauma-passed-healing/.

ENDNOTES

1   Richard I. Kirkland Jr., "Should You Leave It All to the Children?," Fortune, September 29, 1986, https://money.cnn.com/magazines/fortune/fortune_archive/1986/09/29/68098/index.htm.

2   "Inheriting a Fortune: Overcoming the Challenges of Sudden Wealth Syndrome," FasterCapital, last modified June 2, 2024, https://fastercapital.com/content/Inheriting-a-Fortune--Overcoming-the-Challenges-of-Sudden-Wealth-Syndrome.html; "Sudden Wealth Syndrome," Money Meaning & Choices Institute, accessed September 4, 2024, https://www.mmcinstitute.com/about-2/sudden-wealth-syndrome/.

3   Peter Cole, "The Psychological Dynamics of Inherited Wealth," Street Directory, accessed September 4, 2024, https://www.streetdirectory.com/travel_guide/143282/how_to_grow_wealth/the_psychological_dynamics_of_inherited_wealth.html.

4   Judy Lin Walsh, and Stephen Salley, "The Inheritance Effect," Banyan Global, accessed September 4, 2024, https://banyan.global/ideas/the-inheritance-effect/.

5   Walsh and Salley, "The Inheritance Effect."

6   Walsh and Salley, "The Inheritance Effect."

7   Walsh and Salley, "The Inheritance Effect."

8   Walsh and Salley, "The Inheritance Effect."

9   Walsh and Salley, "The Inheritance Effect."

10 Walsh and Salley, "The Inheritance Effect."

11 Arthur T. Vanderbilt II, Fortune's Children: The Fall of the House of Vanderbilt (William Morrow, 2001), 280.

12 Walsh and Salley, "The Inheritance Effect."

13 Walsh and Salley, "The Inheritance Effect."

14 Walsh and Salley, "The Inheritance Effect."

15 Walsh and Salley, "The Inheritance Effect."

16 Leo Sands, "For Mega-Rich Heirs, the Anxieties That Drive 'Succession' Are All Too Real," Washington Post, last modified May 31, 2023, https://www.washingtonpost.com/wellness/2023/05/30/succession-wealth-family-life-psychologists/.

17 "Inheriting a Fortune"; "Sudden Wealth Syndrome."

18 Charlotte Edmonds, "Here's How Much Money the Average NFL Player Makes in 2022," NBC Sports Philadelphia, July 29, 2022, https://www.nbcsportsphiladelphia.com/nfl/philadelphia-eagles/heres-how-much-money-the-average-nfl-player-makes-in-2022/250699/.

19 Pablo S. Torre, "How (and Why) Athletes Go Broke," Sports Illustrated, March 23, 2009, https://vault.si.com/vault/2009/03/23/how-and-why-athletes-go-broke.

20 Daniel Kahneman and Angus Deaton, "High Income Improves Evaluation of Life But Not Emotional Well-Being," Proceedings of the National Academy of Sciences of the United States of America 107, no. 38 (2010): 16489–16493, https://doi.org/10.1073/pnas.1011492107.

21 Grant E. Donnelly et al., "The Amount and Source of Millionaires' Wealth (Moderately) Predict Their Happiness," Personality & Social Psychology Bulletin 44, no. 5 (2018): 684–699, https://doi.org/10.1177/0146167217744766.

22 Donelly et al., "Amount and Source."

23 Jonathan Gardner and Andrew J. Oswald, "Money and Mental Wellbeing: A Longitudinal Study of Medium-sized Lottery Wins," Journal of Health Economics 26, no. 1 (2007): 49–60, https://doi.org/10.1016/j.jhealeco.2006.08.004.

24 Donnelly et al., "Amount and Source."

25 David Miller, "The Common Misconceptions About a Wealthy Upbringing," Psychology Today, July 11, 2018, https://www.psychologytoday.com/us/blog/the-human-side-finance/201807/the-common-misconceptions-about-wealthy-upbringing; Lee Ying Shan, "'Wealth Can Be Pretty Isolating': Problems That Rich People Face, According to Therapists," CNBC, May 13, 2024, https://www.cnbc.com/2024/05/14/problems-that-rich-people-face-according-to-therapists-.html.

26 Mihaly Csikszentmihalyi, "If We Are So Rich, Why Aren't We Happy?" American Psychologist 54, no. 10 (1999): 821–827, https://doi.org/10.1037/0003-066X.54.10.821.

27 Feld Hyde, "Affluenza: The Disease of Inherited Wealth," August 2019, https://dfhlaw.com/wp-content/uploads/2019/08/affluenza-disease-inherited-wealth.pdf.

28 Hyde, "Affluenza."

29 Cole, "Psychological Dynamics"; "Sudden Wealth Syndrome"; Walsh and Salley, "The Inheritance Effect"; Izbassar Assylzhan et al., "Intelligent System for Assessing University Student Personality Development and Career Readiness," Procedia Computer Science 231 (2024): 779–785, https://doi.org/10.48550/arXiv.2308.15620; "Inheriting a Fortune"; James Chen, "Sudden Wealth Syndrome (SWS): Definition, Causes, and Treatment," Investopedia, last modified September 1, 2024, https://www.investopedia.com/terms/s/suddenwealthsyndrome.asp.

30 Joyce Marter, "Financial Trauma: Symptoms, Causes, & How to Cope," Choosing Therapy, May 3, 2024, https://www.choosingtherapy.com/financial-trauma/.

31 Gina Ryder, "What Is Genetic Trauma?" PsychCentral, February 18, 2022, https://psychcentral.com/health/genetic-trauma.

32 Tiffany Curtis, "How Generational Trauma Affects Your Finances and How to Heal," NerdWallet, November 2, 2022, https://www.nerdwallet.com/article/finance/generational-trauma.

33 Reshawna Chapple, "What Is Generational Trauma? Signs, Causes, & How to Heal," Talkspace, February 2, 2023, https://www.talkspace.com/blog/generational-trauma/.

34 "Epigenetics," Psychology Today, accessed September 4, 2024, https://www.psychologytoday.com/us/basics/epigenetics.

35 "Epigenetics."

36 Chapple, "What Is Generational Trauma?"

37 Curtis, "How Generational Trauma Affects Your Finances."

38 Curtis, "How Generational Trauma Affects Your Finances."

39 Curtis, "How Generational Trauma Affects Your Finances."

40 Chapple, "What Is Generational Trauma?"

41 Chapple, "What Is Generational Trauma?"

42 Curtis, "How Generational Trauma Affects Your Finances."

43 Chapple, "What Is Generational Trauma?"

44 Chapple, "What Is Generational Trauma?"

45 Jeremy E. Sherman, "How the Rich Cope with Shame About Their Unfair Advantage," Psychology Today, September 17, 2019, https://www.psychologytoday.com/us/blog/ambigamy/201909/how-the-rich-cope-shame-about-their-unfair-advantage.

46 "'My Trust Fund Made Me Miserable': Lucky Relatives Set to Inherit Millions Reveal How Their Wealth Makes Them Feel 'Guilty and Isolated,'" Daily Mail, last modified August 18, 2018, https://www.dailymail.co.uk/news/article-6071429/The-dark-guilty-lonely-having-million-dollar-trust-fund.html.

47 "'My Trust Fund.'"

48 "'My Trust Fund.'"

49 "'My Trust Fund.'"

50 "'My Trust Fund.'"

51 "'My Trust Fund.'"

52 Derek Hegen, "How to Think About Wealth and Guilt," Meaningful Money, October 1, 2020, https://www.meaningfulmoney.life/post/wealth-guilt.

53 "'My Trust Fund.'"

54 David, interview with the author.

55 Eve Glicksman, "Your Brain on Guilt and Shame," BrainFacts.org, September 12, 2019, https://www.brainfacts.org/thinking-sensing-and-behaving/emotions-stress-and-anxiety/2019/your-brain-on-guilt-and-shame-091219.

56 Glicksman, "Your Brain on Guilt and Shame."

57 Jena Field, "The Science Behind Guilt and Shame," The Monkey Therapist, accessed September 4, 2024, https://themonkeytherapist.com/science-behind-guilt-shame/.

58 Field, "Science Behind Guilt and Shame."

59 Field, "Science Behind Guilt and Shame."

60 Field, "Science Behind Guilt and Shame."

61 Field, "Science Behind Guilt and Shame."

62 Ratner et al., "Daily Adolescent Purposefulness"; Judy Reynolds, "Unleashing the Power of Purpose: Leading a Life of Passion and Success," Opening Gates, July 14, 2023, https://openinggates.com/unleashing-the-power-of-purpose-leading-a-life-of-passion-and-success/; Serena, "The Power of Purpose: A Guided Journey to a Fulfilling Life," Horizon Hub, Medium, February 4, 2024, https://medium.com/horizon-hub/the-power-of-purpose-a-guided-journey-to-a-fulfilling-life-9c5c6d711be7; Emiliana R. Simon-Thomas, "How Strong Is Your Sense of Purpose in Life?," Greater Good Magazine, April 11, 2022, https://greatergood.berkeley.edu/article/item/how_strong_is_your_sense_of_purpose_in_life.

63 Simon-Thomas, "Sense of Purpose."

64 Simon-Thomas, "Sense of Purpose."

65 Patrick L. Hill, and Nicholas A. Turiano, "Purpose in Life as a Predictor of Mortality Across Adulthood," Psychological Science 25, no. 7 (2014): 1482–1486, https://doi.org/10.1177/0956797614531799.

66 Hyde, "Affluenza."

67 Patrick L. Hill et al., "Collegiate Purpose Orientations and Well-Being in Early and Middle Adulthood," Journal of Applied Developmental Psychology 31, no. 2 (2010): 173–179, https://doi.org/10.1016/j.appdev.2009.12.001.

68 Matthew J. Bundick et al., "The Contours of Purpose Beyond the Self in Midlife and Later Life," Applied Developmental Science 25, no. 1 (2019): 62–82, https://doi.org/10.1080/10888691.2018.1531718.

69 Nadia [pseudonym], Zoom interview with author, March 20, 2024.

70 "Infographic: The Family Business—Successes and Obstacles," Score, June 13, 2024, https://www.score.org/resource/infographic/infographic-family-business—successes-and-obstacles.

71 Hyde, "Affluenza."